Spanish visual culture

Manchester University Press

Spanish visual culture
Cinema, television, internet

Paul Julian Smith

Manchester University Press
Manchester and New York

distributed exclusively in the USA by Palgrave

Published by Manchester University Press
Oxford Road, Manchester M13 9NR, UK
and Room 400, 175 Fifth Avenue, New York, NY 10010, USA
www.manchesteruniversitypress.co.uk

Distributed exclusively in the USA by
Palgrave, 175 Fifth Avenue, New York,
NY 10010, USA

Distributed exclusively in Canada by
UBC Press, University of British Columbia, 2029 West Mall,
Vancouver, BC, Canada V6T 1Z2

British Library Cataloguing-in-Publication Data
A catalogue record for this book is available from the British Library

Library of Congress Cataloging-in-Publication Data applied for

ISBN   07190 75173 *hardback*
EAN   97807190 75179

ISBN   07190 7536x *paperback*
EAN   97807190 75360

First published 2006

15 14 13 12 11 10 09 08 07 06   10 9 8 7 6 5 4 3 2 1

Typeset by
D R Bungay Associates, Burghfield, Berks

Printed in Great Britain by
Biddles, King's Lynn

Contents

To London, in memory of 7.7.2005

Grey city. Stubbornly implanted,
Taken so for granted for a thousand years.
Stay, city. Smokily enchanted,
Cradle of our memories and hopes and fears.

(Noel Coward)

List of illustrations

Acknowledgements

My thanks to the faculty and students of the Universities of Cambridge and Stanford, California, where I taught while writing this book. Chapter 3 could not have been written without the archive of movida material left by Dr Peter C. Scales and kindly delivered to me by Jo Labanyi. I would also like to thank the Spanish friends who sent copies of TV shows they had taped for me. Earlier versions of material from this book were first published in *Hispanic Research Journal*, 3 (2002), 277–86; *Journal of Latin American Cultural Studies*, 12 (2003), 389–400; *Journal of Romance Studies*, 4 (2004), 91–102; and *MLN*, 119 (2004), 363–75. While every effort has been made to contact copyright holders for the visual material reproduced here the author welcomes corrections and additions.

Introduction:
three media, three themes

Three media: cinema, television, internet

In a recent article Andrea Noble discusses the current turn to visual culture in relation to Latin American studies ('Notes'). While she welcomes the new academic attention to the visual, which is held to correspond to shifts in the nature of a society that has moved from the text to the image, she also questions the validity of this general debate for the specific case of Latin America. Noble argues that it is only if the textual is restricted to alphabetical writing that it can be contrasted with the visual. In Amerindian cultures that used painted signs or knotted strings as forms of notation, the distinction cannot hold. Moreover the visual turn is held in general debate to be a very recent, even postmodern development. Yet the question of text and image (book and ideogram) was clearly central to the cultural struggles that followed the Spanish conquest. Noble suggests, then, that we should question both the unthinking opposition between textual and visual culture and the application of a "visual turn," perceived as universal, to nations with very different cultural histories.

The argument holds true for contemporary Spain as well. It has sometimes been argued that Spain passed directly from a premodern oral culture (in which, we might add, the imagistic component was unusually rich) to a postmodern visual culture, leapfrogging the intermediate textual stage (Graham and Labanyi 1995, 409). Certainly, as we shall see, Spanish rates of newspaper readership have always been very low, barely reaching the index of a developed nation. Moreover the discursive wars over contemporary Spanish culture have tended to focus on the visual element, which is often held to be dangerous. In his "critical history" of the transition to democracy, published as early as 1980, Juan Luis Cebrián, the editor of the hegemonic daily *El País*, concludes his call for the construction of a new Spain with an unexpected quote from Ramón Pérez de Ayala in 1917:

Yo declaro mi amor por aquellos países como los Estados Unidos del Norte de América, en donde no se ven jamás trajes llamativos, ya por lo crudo de los colores ya por la lobreguez talar. (Cebrián 1980, 145)

I declare my love for those countries such as the United States of America, where showy clothes are not seen, whether they are brightly coloured garments or those which gloomily reach down to the ankles.

Both the flamboyant military uniform and the ostentatiously dowdy clerical garb are thus to be avoided. While this pro-Americanism would be difficult to imagine in contemporary Spain, the moral remains current. For Pérez de Ayala it is those countries where clothing does not improperly call attention to itself which decide global affairs and the course of human life. It is a suspicion of the visual which became commonplace in the decade which followed Cebrián's study of the transition, when the cultural explosion known as the movida (see chapter 3) seemed to exemplify contemporary Spanish culture. Cebrián himself wrote that the architects of the movida (such as Pedro Almodóvar, discussed in chapter 1 of this book) were so busy with the "façade" that they forgot to build the house (Cebrián 1987, 47). Other commentators decried postmodern Spain as the definitive society of the spectacle, all surface and no substance (Subirats 1988).

Such claims need to be carefully contextualized. After all, postmodernism is often held to be a general condition and cannot be uniquely applied to Spain. If we look more closely at the three visual media that I treat in this book (cinema, television, and internet), we come across some interesting contradictions which work against both journalistic and academic commonplaces.

While critical commentary on Spanish culture after the rightist Partido Popular came to power in 1996 is often negative, economic and social indicators suggest that conditions were improving for the Spanish population. In *Spain at a Glance 2001*, William Chislett notes that Spain's rate of economic growth was consistently above the European Union average (Chislett 2000, 12) and that Spain was moving up the tables of business competitiveness and UN human development (*ibid.*, 21, 23). These trends seemed to carry over into visual media such as film. Bullish accounts of Spanish film in the 1990s stress a "new resurgence" (Benavent 2000, 11) based on the incorporation of younger filmmakers, new cinematic forms, a more youthful audience, and a more efficient mode of production (Heredero and Santamarina 2002, 13). In chapter 2 I consider one example of this renewal: the emergence of a Spanish version of the "youth movie."

The official figures appear to speak for themselves: while the number of cinemas fell from 1,322 (1991) to 1,254 (2001) the number of screens rose from 1,802 (1989) to 3,747 (2001) and the annual frequency of cinema visits per head of population from *c.* 2.01 to a high 3.66 (*European Cinema Yearbook*). Admissions to multiplexes rose rapidly as a percentage of total cinema visits (from 29.8% in 1998 to 53.4% in 2001). But, surprisingly, this did not seem to harm local films in their booming local market: the share of domestic movies rose from *c.* 7.3% in 1989 to 17.9% in 2001, while US films fell in the same period from 73.0% to 62.2%. In the same year two Spanish films were seen by more Spaniards than any Hollywood blockbuster: the supernatural thriller *The Others* by wunderkind Alejandro Amenábar (who is discussed in chapter 6) and Santiago Segura's coarse comedy *Torrente 2* gained audiences of over six and five million respectively in a population of barely forty million.

Other films in the domestic top ten were Vicente Aranda's historical epic *Juana la Loca* (discussed in chapter 5 of this book) and Julio Medem's erotic art movie *Lucía y el sexo* (*Sex and Lucía*), both seen by over one million spectators. Guillermo del Toro's *El espinazo del diablo* (*The Devil's Backbone*) (an example of the Mexico-Spanish co-productions discussed in chapter 8) and Achero Mañas's *El bola* (*Pellet*) (a social realist drama on child abuse) also featured in the list. The national slate was thus as varied in genre as it was successful at the box office. Further statistics show the increasingly urban nature of Spanish cinema audiences, with the top three cities accounting for only 12.9% of the population but 23.2% of the gross box office; and, paradoxically perhaps, an increase in feature film production (from 48 in 1989 to 106 in 2001) which coincides with a decrease in government subsidy for the audiovisual sector (reduced from over 200 million pesetas in 1996 to virtually zero in 2001). In chapter 8 of this book we will see a similar dynamic at work in Mexico.

Some academics, both abroad and in Spain, have been sceptical about this critical and industrial resurgence. In her *Spanish National*

Cinema, Núria Triana-Toribio (2003) suggests there is a certain complicity between Spanish critics such as Heredero and "quality" filmmakers such as Medem: Spanish cinema is believed by critics to require a bona fide auteur like Medem in order to reinforce traditional boundaries between high and low culture, to win international prestige at festivals, and to "directly engage with notions of Spanishness" (*ibid.*, 149). And as the financial figures turned negative once more in 2002 there was much renewed talk of a "crisis" in Spanish cinema. The most radical critics again reject such a notion, claiming that the cyclical notion of "crisis" is invented and promoted by the self-interested professionals of the film industry in years when their production fails to connect with the Spanish audience.

Josep Lluís Fecé and Cristina Pujol (2003) suggest that even the supposed "successes" of 2002 are fallacious. *Los lunes al sol* (*Mondays in the Sun*, a prize-winning social realist feature on unemployment) was, they claim, a "media event" created by critics (such as Heredero again) who, aware of its many cinematic defects, still praised it to the skies simply for having tackled a serious political subject (*ibid.*, 157). Inversely *El otro lado de la cama* (*The Other Side of the Bed*) a feel-good romantic comedy with music) is a phenomenon created by the publicity process through an incipient Spanish star system which is parasitic on television: two of its protagonists, Paz Vega and Guillermo Toledo, both made their names on long-running Tele 5 sitcom *7 Vidas* (*Seven* or *Nine Lives*, which I discuss in chapter 2 of this book) and their film characters are unintelligible without knowledge of this background (*ibid.*, 159).

Another critic who has stressed the interdependency of film and television in Spain is Chris Perriam (2003), whose book length study of Spanish stars engages meticulously with their small screen work. Indeed it is clear from the documentation given by Perriam that as the film profile of an established star such as Imanol Arias fades, his TV profile soars. Arias is currently the star of the most popular drama on Televisión Española, the long running nostalgic family series *Cuéntame cómo pasó* (*Tell Me How It Happened*) discussed in chapter 1 of this book).

As in the case of cinema, it is difficult to separate the vicissitudes of funding from the content of Spanish television. In his *European Television in the Digital Age*, Stylianos Papathanassopoulos (2002) shows how Spanish TV has been in the vanguard of recent and current industrial change. In 1982 Spain was the third country in Europe after the UK and Italy to deregulate its terrestrial television (*ibid.*, 15), thus opening the way for a multichannel environment. It also led the way with "proximate" TV, i.e. regional centres for public corporations such as TVE and local channels (*ibid.*, 25) and in 1997 became the third country in the world to introduce digital terrestrial television (*ibid.*, 48). Meanwhile the audience share of the public channels declined more sharply in Spain than in any of the big five Euro countries (Germany, France, UK, and Italy), from 45.7% in 1992 to 33.1% in 2000 (*ibid.*, 67). The funding system is also unique in the EU. Only Spain (and Portugal) fund public broadcasting through state subsidy and advertising, without a licence fee (*ibid.*, 69). It is thus unsurprising both that private channels Tele 5 and Antena 3 lodged the first complaint in the EU against the anti-competitive funding of a public broadcaster (*ibid.*, 74) and that RTVE is severely and increasingly burdened with debt (*ibid.*, 78).

Less expected is the relationship between television and politics in Spain. Spaniards use television for information more than some other Europeans (Spain: 70% vs France: 59%); and they seek information from the press less than others (Spain: 28% vs UK: 50% [Papathanassopoulos 2002, 126]). In 1999 they also pronounced themselves much more favourable to the way democracy works in their country: 21% of Spaniards are "very satisfied," compared to 7% of the French, and just 3% of Italians (*ibid.*, 129). Contradicting the common view that Spaniards quickly grew disillusioned with democracy, at the millennium they volunteer the highest level of trust in government of the Euro big five (*ibid.*, 130). Public trust in the media is also relatively high: 62% in the press and 66% in TV, as opposed to EU 15 averages of 49% and 67% respectively (*ibid.*, 134).

According to Papathanassopoulos, Spanish media have also moved with the rest of Europe "from the general to the particular" in their development of thematic channels (2002, 149). For example, when CNN began its Spanish-language service in Spain it made sure 80% of content was generated in Europe (*ibid.*, 177). This degree of localization is also found in sports, music, and children's channels run by multinational interests (*ibid.*, 194, 222, 231). As we shall see, the theme of "location" is a central one to this book.

Papathanassopoulos ends with a warning of the deepening divide between informational "haves" and "have-nots" in Europe (2002, 248); and he notes that "the European viewer has gone from being a silent citizen in the state monopoly era to a valuable consumer in the digital era of private oligopolies" (*ibid.*, 251). While, as we shall see in the first two chapters of this book, both private and public networks are still able to mobilize national audiences around must-see TV dramas, it is instructive to compare current data on the new consumers with those of other media in Spain. The AIMC, a commercial research body, tells us that for the period October 2002 to May 2003, the market penetration of media was as follows: weekly filmgoers 9.3%; daily newspaper readers 39%; and daily television viewers 90.7%. These audiences are given a profile according to sex, age, and social class. Newspaper readers tend in Spain to be of disproportionately higher class, as do filmgoers, given the increased price of tickets. More interesting is the gender profile. While 49% of men read a newspaper, only 29.6% of women do so. Filmgoers are also slightly out of sync: 10.0% of men as opposed to 8.7% of women. By far the most balanced medium for all three categories is television, with near equal proportions of men and women, young and old, rich and poor tuning in every day (there is a slight dip in the 20s which coincides with peek filmgoing years). It thus follows that television production will be much more closely related to the general national taste than will feature films. Incidentally, women are less interested in radio and more avid consumers of magazines than men, suggesting a greater bias towards visual culture. In chapter 2 of this book I consider a major illustrated magazine, *La Luna de Madrid* (*The Moon of Madrid*), whose visual style is widely held to embody the spirit of the movida.

Internet use is also heavily gendered. In chapter 7 I reconstruct in some detail Manuel Castells' scattered but definitive account of the relationship between the information economy and Spain (and Latin America). More recent figures from the AIMC again suggest that internet penetration is rapidly rising, from 2.7% in 1997 to 25.2% in the first half of 2003. However this breaks down as 30.3% of men and 20.4% of women. This situation may change, given the rapid rise in internet access at home, as opposed to work (female unemployment remains high in Spain). However it suggests that the efforts by artists such as Marisa González (whom I also discuss in chapter 7) to address women's issues on the Web, however obliquely, are especially important. According to the Sociedad General de Autores y Editores (2003, 439) the TV channels whose drama I found particularly innovative (TVE-1 and Tele 5) are also disproportionately attractive to female audiences.

One final factor affecting the Spanish audiovisual sector is nationality. As is well known, it is increasingly hard to allocate a national origin to any cultural product. Amenábar's *The Others*, filmed in Spain and with a Spanish crew, was shot in English and with an Australian star (Nicole Kidman). A US–Spanish co-production, it was received in both countries as a local film. Long an importer of television, Spain now also exports formats originated at home, and has recently become a major producer of children's animation (Papathanassopoulos 2002, 240). At an exhibition of Catalan web art held in Barcelona's Santa Mónica gallery, and inaugurated by politicians of the Generalitat who have long campaigned for the "normalization" of the Catalan language, the great majority of the text used in the art works was written in English, a lingua franca both on the internet and in a Spain divided by linguistic conflict. The web artist known as Zush (whom I discuss in chapter 7) solves the problem of choosing between Catalan, Castilian, and English by inventing his own private language and script, the exotically named "Evrugo" and "Asura."

Spain's unique relation to Latin America is vital here. Spain is the biggest direct investor in the continent and Telefónica, its communications giant, is the biggest Spanish company in Latin America. Coincidentally Telefónica also funded the project by artist Marisa González which I also consider in chapter 7. William Chislett notes that "Spanish publishers were pioneers in the internationalization of Spanish companies" (2003, 185). These include Grupo Prisa which prints editions of *El País* in Mexico and Argentina (*ibid.*, 188). The tourism and satellite communications sectors are also influential (*ibid.*, 192). Transatlantic traffic is thus particularly marked in the cultural and media sectors.

In a survey of Latin American cinema in the 1990s published as an afterword to the second edition of *Magical Reels*, John King (2000, 253) cites Nestor García Canclini's question "Will there be a Latin American cinema in the year 2000?" García Canclini's work was sponsored by the Mexican film institute IMCINE, then vigorously promoting local cinema production. In the same spirit King writes that, in an age of globalization, "the national is not the site of retrograde nostalgia, but the bedrock of any possible development of cinema" (*ibid.*, 255). What King could not have foreseen was the "new Mexican wave" of such films as Alejandro González Iñárritu's *Amores perros* and Alfonso Cuarón's *Y tu mamá también* (which I discuss in chapter 8), successful features made without state funding and, indeed, by directors and producers openly hostile to the paternalism of IMCINE.

Yet even here in films 100% locally funded and intended for the home market, there is a strong Spanish element – the presence of lead actresses from the Peninsula in both films. A special issue of trade paper *Screen International* (19–25 September 2003) argued that, with the successes of directors like Almodóvar and González Iñárritu and actors like Gael García Bernal across the region, "Latin American and Spanish producers [were] turn[ing] to each other to overcome financial difficulties" (13). One claimed that "If we do it right, Spain could become the gateway between Europe, the US and Latin America" (*ibid.*, 14). Like the fluid network structures of the internet, cinematic co-productions thus suggest the interconnection of the economic and the aesthetic in cultural forms that transcend the nation state.

Three themes: emotion, location, nostalgia

There is only one bus a day to the Valle de los Caídos (Valley of the Fallen), the monumental cross and crypt built by Francisco Franco to commemorate the Nationalist dead of the Civil War. On a splendid September afternoon in 2003 it is half empty. As we drive up the lengthy monumental approach we pass only two cars. On arrival the funicular railway to the summit is closed and the cafe shuttered. The great empty terrace, high in the Guadarrama sierra, seems like the remnant of some lost ancient civilization, as resonant and as enigmatic as Stonehenge. In the shadowy Basilica, hewn 260 metres into the bare rock, buckets collect water which drips through the gold mosaic ceiling. Franco's tomb, opposite that of José Antonio, founder of the fascist Falange party, is bare but for a single bouquet of white lilies.

Madrid itself is full of other "places of memory," to use the formula of French cultural historian Pierre Nora (1984–92). One that springs to mind is the Panteón de Hombres Ilustres (Pantheon of Illustrious Men), a neo-Classical collection of tombs near Atocha Station, honouring now forgotten nineteenth-century worthies. But the Valle de los Caídos is especially resonant and not just because of the overwhelming visual load that comes from its sheer size (the cross is 150 metres high). First, the Valle engages the visitor's emotions quite directly: whatever one's response to this blatantly fascist architecture, it is surely designed to work on the feelings more than the intellect. Secondly, it is a unique location: the very difficulty in reaching the Valle reinforces its intense and disquieting spirit of place. Finally, it poses the question of nostalgia in contemporary Spain. I shall argue in this book that, contrary to critical consensus and in spite of the neglect of the Valle, contemporary Spanish culture is highly engaged by the past: from TV drama set in the 1960s to heritage movies set in the 15th century, via novels which recycle the 1980s.

While Alberto Medina deplores the neglect of the Valle as a sign of historical amnesia, I would celebrate that neglect as proof of Spanish culture's successful engagement with or working through the past. I thus try to examine nostalgia sympathetically in this book (to read it for its complex fusion of time, space, and feeling). But the lack of nostalgia for the dictatorship and its monuments is surely a positive phenomenon. The many Russian tourists I encountered that September afternoon at the Valle would no doubt contrast its near emptiness with the shrines to Stalin, which remain magnetic attractions for those ex-Soviet citizens who mourn the certainties of totalitarianism.

If, then, cultural studies has seen a visual turn, then it has also registered a new and serious interest in emotions. In the first two chapters of this book I draw on two influential theorists of the emotions in order to reread Spanish cinema and television: moral philosopher Martha Nussbaum and oral historian Luisa Passerini. Nussbaum's major contention is that emotions cannot easily be separated from ideas and that they thus have a moral and political dimension to which we should pay respectful attention. I argue that this is also the case with Almodóvar's *Hable con ella* (*Talk to Her*), a film which invites an emotional participation which transcends its overt narrative; and TVE's *Cuéntame cómo pasó* (*Tell Me How It Happened*), a series drama set in the late Francoist period, which encourages modern viewers to understand Spanish history by locating it within the private domestic sphere. For Luisa Passerini, also, feeling is inseparable from politics. Her work on Italian fascism has shown how families created personal narratives which reconciled themselves to intolerable public violence. In chapter 2 I read top-rated Spanish television drama as a parallel kind of affective engagement with politics. While *Médico de familia* (*Family Doctor*), a notoriously domestic show, subtly introduced Spaniards to changes such as suburbanization and even immigration, *7 Vidas* (*Seven* or *Nine Lives*), a smart, urban sitcom, reconciles them to new de facto families: consensual groupings of friends that can include such groups as older single people and lesbians.

Emotion is inseparable from location. In the third chapter I read three different versions of what remains the quintessential cultural event of post-Franco Spain: the movida madrileña. Drawing on British cultural geographers I argue that the city can be a space for an informal democratic process which transcends parliamentary politics. Far from being a failure, then, the movida can be read as a laboratory for social change which remains ongoing. I contrast *La Luna de Madrid*, the large-format magazine of the period which both reflected and fostered the movida, with an oral history on the same subject published a decade later and an elegiac novel which cast a nostalgic, but critical, glance over a now mythical period for readers at the turn of the century.

Chapter 4 continues this investigation of location, tracing the process by which a US-derived genre (the youth movie) was anchored in the urban geography of Madrid. *Historias del Kronen* was one of the most successful films of its year, as was costume drama *Juana la Loca*, the subject of chapter 5. Here too location shooting, this time in historical sites also exploited by tourism, is a vital part of the film's attraction. Nostalgia for Spain's heroic past is countered by an attempt to appeal to the youthful contemporary audience. The Anglo-American heritage picture is thus (like the youth movie) adapted for the particular profile of Spanish spectators. In the sixth chapter I focus on another rare case: the thriller *Abre los ojos* (*Open Your Eyes*), remade by Hollywood as *Vanilla Sky*. Once more the differing parts played by location (Madrid and New

York respectively) point up the particularity of a Spanish visual style which, ironically perhaps, has now adopted some of the classic Hollywood conventions (such as narrative causality and economy of means) which have been abandoned by many current US filmmakers.

The last two chapters further investigate the notion of location, treating the Web as virtual space for Spanish art and the transatlantic traffic in what the trade press now calls "Latin" films. The continuing importance of physical location, even in these contexts, is reconfirmed by technological trends. On 13 May 2003 *The Economist* published a report on "The Revenge of Geography." Far from embracing the much heralded "death of distance," the new tendency is to "link places on the internet to places in the real world, stitching together the supposedly separate virtual and physical worlds." These commercial "geolocation services" can perhaps be read as parallel to the artistic practices I consider in chapter 7, as "user-generated location-specific content."

What unites all the media and texts studied here (and to which I devote close analysis) is the particular brilliance of their visual culture, from the resonant objects of *Hable con ella* and *Cuéntame*, haloed by memory and desire, to the edgy shooting styles of *Amores perros* and *Y tu mamá también*. Significantly the relation I trace between space and time is explicit in the etymology of nostalgia (literally "return grief"). In both English and Spanish the term was first used for "home sickness," that is to say the desire to go back to a place, not a time. If the past is another country, then Spaniards are frequent visitors. In a typical week which contains no major anniversaries of Spanish historical events (5–11 September 2003), Madrid's *Guía del ocio* (the main listings magazine) offers citizens a choice of Buero Vallejo's *Historia de una escalera* (*History of a Staircase*) in the theatre (the major work by the best known playwright of the Francoist era), *Soldados de Salamina* (*Soldiers of Salamina*) in the cinema (a feature film which crosscuts between the present day and the Civil War era), and major photographic exhibitions on Barcelona in the 1950s and the International Brigades. The cinephile could also enjoy the continuing screenings of films by Francoist directors such as Edgar Neville and Ramón Torrado at the Filmoteca (the same historic repertory house lovingly cited and shown by Almodóvar in *Hable con ella*).

But the clearest sign of the connection between emotion, location, and nostalgia was the season of films inaugurated at the Centro Cultural de la Villa which traced the history of filmmaking in Madrid from the silent era to the present day. Screenings were followed by discussions in which madrileños proved voluble in expressing their personal investments in such films. If, as Papathanassopoulos suggests, European viewers have changed from silent citizens of the state monopoly era to valuable consumers in the digital age, the Spanish case shows that the recent turn to visual culture has a vital potential for the exploration of historical memory.

Works cited

Benavent, Francisco María. *Cine español de los noventa: diccionario de películas, directores, y temático*. Bilbao: Mensajero, 2000.

Cebrián, Juan Luis. *La España que bosteza: apuntes para la historia de la Transición*. Madrid: Taurus, 1980.

— *El tamaño del elefante*. Madrid: Alianza, 1987.

Chislett, William. *Spain at a Glance 2001*. Madrid: Banco Santander Central Hispano, 2000.

— *Spanish Direct Investment in Latin America: Challenges and Opportunities*. Madrid: Real Instituto Elcano, 2003.

Fecé, Lluís and Pujol, Cristina. 'La crisis imaginada de un cine sin público.' In Luis Alonso García (ed.), *Once miradas sobre la crisis y el cine español*. Madrid: Ocho y Medio, 2003, 147–65.

Graham, Helen and Labanyi, Jo. *Spanish Cultural Studies: An Introduction. The Struggle for Modernity*. Oxford: Oxford University Press, 1995.

Guía del ocio: la semana de Madrid. 5–11 September 2003.

Heredero, Carlos F. and Santamarina, Antonio. *Semillas de futuro: cine español 1990–2001*. Madrid: Sociedad Estatal del Nuevo Milenio, 2002.

King, John. *Magical Reels: A History of Cinema in Latin America*. London and New York: Verso, 2000.

Medina Domínguez, Alberto. *Exorcismos de la memoria: políticas y poéticas de la melancolía en la España de la transición*. Madrid: Libertarias, 2001.

Nora, Pierre (ed.). *Les lieux de memoire*. 7 vols. Paris: Gallimard, 1984–92.

Papathanassopoulos, Stylianos. *European Television in the Digital Age: Issues, Dynamics, and Realities.* Cambridge and Oxford: Polity, 2002.

Perriam, Chris. *Stars and Masculinities in Spanish Cinema: From Banderas to Bardem.* Oxford: Oxford University Press, 2003.

Screen International [London] [Special issue on Spanish and Latin American cinema]. 19–25 September 2003.

SGAE. *Anuario SGAE de las artes escénicas, musicales, y audiovisuales.* Madrid: Sociedad General de Autores y Editores and Fundación Autor, 2003.

Subirats, Eduardo. *La cultura como espectáculo.* Mexico: Fondo de Cultura Económica, 1988.

Triana-Toribio, Núria. *Spanish National Cinema.* London and New York: Routledge, 2003.

Electronic sources

AIMC [Asociación de Investigación de Medios de Comunicación]. 'EGM: año móvil octubre 2002–mayo 2003.' 25 September 2003. www.aimc.es/02egm/resumegm203.pdf

The Economist. 'The revenge of geography.' 13 May 2003. www.economist.com

European Cinema Year Book. Accessed 18 December 2003. www.mediasalles.it/yearbook.htm

Noble, Andrea. 'Notes on the "new" visual culture from the perspective of the "new" Latin Americanism.' Accessed 18 December 2003. www.art.man.ac.uk/Lacs/seminars_events/newlatam/papers/noble.htm

1 The emotional imperative: Almodóvar's *Hable con ella (Talk to Her)* and Televisión Española's *Cuéntame cómo pasó (Tell Me How It Happened)*

Emotion as cognition

In *Upheavals of Thought: The Intelligence of Emotions*, Martha C. Nussbaum (2001) offers a broad, deep, and complex account of the relationship between knowledge and feeling. Nussbaum begins with two epigraphs. The first is from Proust. It cites the "geological upheavals" that love caused to take place in the mind of M. de Charlus, which, we are told, "only several days before resembled a plain so flat that ... one could not have discerned an idea sticking up above the ground." Now "a mountain range has abruptly thrust itself into view ... Rage, Jealousy, Curiosity, Envy, Hate, Suffering, Pride, Astonishment, and Love" (unpaginated). The second epigraph is from Freud's "Group Psychology and the Analysis of the Ego." Freud writes: "By being born we have made the step from an absolutely self-sufficient narcissism to the perception of a changing external world and the beginnings of the discovery of objects." This shift is perilous, however: "we cannot endure the new state of affairs for long ... [and] we periodically revert from it, in our sleep, to our former condition of absence of stimulation and avoidance of objects" (unpaginated).

Crucial here are Proust's baptism of the emotions as "ideas" and Freud's proposal that perception and stimulation (the discovery of the world and the pleasure produced by it) are inseparable. Nussbaum's argument, then, is that emotions are "intelligent responses to the perception of value." She continues:

Instead of viewing morality as a system of principles to be grasped by the detached intellect, and emotions as motivations that either support or subvert our choice to act according to principle, we will have to consider emotions as part and parcel of the system of ethical reasoning. (Nussbaum 2001, 1)

As Nussbaum acknowledges herself, such a project is highly perilous. Emotions are not to be considered as "immune from rational criticism;" and they should even be regarded with some suspicion "given their specific content and the nature of their history" (Nussbaum 2001, 2). But it is precisely this history that Nussbaum seeks to elaborate in the multiple, but parallel, spheres of society, psyche, and culture. Broadly speaking she argues for social construction and variation in emotion (at one point arguing for a distinctively "American death" in the notorious weepy *Terms of Endearment* [*ibid.*, 165–9]), traces the emergence of emotions in infancy (relating them, as in Freud, to the subject–object relation [*ibid.*, 174, 238]), and argues for the privileged role of artistic expression (especially music and literature) in suggesting a "ladder of love" that has democratic uses as "an education for compassionate citizenship" (*ibid.*, 432). Working through anthropology, psychoanalysis, and cultural criticism, Nussbaum thus arrives at a final question: "How can love reform itself, so as not to be excessively needy, vengeful, or partial, and so as to be supportive of general social compassion, reciprocity, and respect for individuality?" (*ibid.*, 481). It is a question also posed urgently by and in recent Spanish audiovisual narrative.

Nussbaum barely considers film or television, although she does cite Proust's magic lantern as a simile for emotion: "colouring the room one is actually in with the intense images of other objects, other stories" (Nusbaum 2001, 178). Many readers will find her discussion of mourning and melancholia (especially her brave account of the circumstances of her own mother's death) particularly moving and illuminating here. In this first chapter I explore two recent works that, I argue, suggest with unusual colour and intensity that emotion is a form of cognition and love a kind of intelligence. The first is Almodóvar's recent feature film *Hable con ella* (2002), which proposes that knowledge (of self and others) comes only through caretaking of individuals. The second is TVE's most successful current series *Cuéntame cómo pasó* (2001–), a family drama set in the late 1960s. A "quality" product festooned with prizes (like Almodóvar's recent films), *Cuéntame* exploits the unique temporal and spatial matrix of TV to show that it is only by passing through the private (passional) sphere that we can come to know the public (dispassionate) history of the nation. What I call the "emotional imperative" in these two works (the urgent requirement to speak and to tell) is thus inseparable from the intellectual goal of understanding subjects and institutions.

Hable con ella: the mourning of beauty

Almodóvar's progressive acquisition of cultural distinction, which makes his work now loom up as a mountain range in the flat plain of Spanish cinema, is well documented. While I wrote in 1994 that Almodóvar had been "punished by male critics for placing himself so consistently on the side of the woman (on the side of sentiment and of spectacle)" (Smith 1994, 101) by 2002 I was exploring the "increased measures of both aestheticization and social commentary" that had brought him hard won magisterial status (Smith 2002, 153). Hable con ella is a clear extension of this process, with the director's characteristic "auto-interview" making reference to the great (male) masters of European cinema such as Rossellini and Antonioni who spawned the most intellectual practices and theories of film (Almodóvar official Spanish website). It is perhaps no accident that Hable focuses, unusually, on male friendship: the odd couple of loquacious male nurse Benigno (Illustration 1) and strong and silent travel writer Marco. The female protagonists, bullfighter Lydia and ballerina Alicia, lie comatose for most of the 110 minutes running time. The intricate plotting of the film is clearly the result of conscious, even self-conscious, deliberation. Thus amongst the ironic symmetries and ironies of a story that flows backwards and forwards in time are: the tripartite division of the film by intertitles into the story of three couples (Benigno and Alicia; Marco and Lydia; Marco and Alicia); Marco's tending to his mute lover, just as Benigno has tended to his; Lydia falling victim to the bull, just as Alicia did to the (unseen) traffic accident; and, finally, Marco taking up the position of Benigno, spying from his friend's window on a miraculously reborn Alicia. Where previous Almodóvar plots spun out of control (echoing what Nussbaum calls the "unpredictable and disorderly operation [of emotions] in daily life" [2001, 2]), Hable makes masterful use of cinematic resources such as mise en scène and music to reduce "messy and ungovernable" feelings (Nussbaum, again [*ibid.*, 16]) to apparently rational control.

If we look at the film's promotion and reception, however, we see that *Hable* is by no means seen and shown in terms of detached intellect. Almodóvar claims that he seeks rather to combine transparency of form with frankness of emotion. And he stresses the direct connection between aesthetics and feeling. Using a characteristic high culture reference he claims:

Creo que fue Cocteau quien dijo que la "belleza" puede resultar dolorosa. Supongo que se refería a la belleza de las personas, yo creo que las situaciones que entrañan momentos de belleza inesperados y extraordinarios pueden hacerte saltar las lágrimas, lágrimas que se parecen más al dolor que al placer. Lágrimas que ocupan en nuestros ojos el lugar de los ausentes. (Almodóvar official Spanish website)

I believe it was Cocteau who said that "beauty" can be painful. I suppose he was talking about the beauty of people, [but] I think that situations which bear within them unexpected and extraordinary moments of beauty can make tears spring to the eyes, tears that are closer to pain than pleasure. Tears that take the place of absent people in our eyes.

If art schools us in feeling it is thus because the grief it inspires is a kind of mourning, a precious substitute for the loss of objects which in Freud's words (cited by Nussbaum once more) cast a "shadow over the ego" (2001, 174).

But *Hable* is also about ethics. In Almodóvar's own texts once more he stresses how through "la larga convalescencia de las heridas provocadas por la pasión" ("the long convalescence from the wounds caused by passion") monologue can be replaced by dialogue, isolation by intimacy. Explicitly, the emotional imperative is that we attempt communication with the other even in the most reduced and tragic of circumstances. Like Freud's infant, Almodóvar's women have retreated from intensely stimulating and perilous perception of objects into the self-sufficient narcissism of coma. Almodóvar compares Benigno's ceaseless prattle to the unconscious Alicia to his own childish retelling of movie plots to his uncomprehending family. Cinema can thus be read both as the shadow that threatens and annihilates the self and the magic lantern that illuminates it with the traces of absent others, uncannily intensified and luridly coloured.

Critics generally took up Almodóvar's invitation to fuse emotion and cognition, feeling and knowledge. While some acknowledged their own tears as frankly as Marco in the opening sequence of the film, others (or sometimes the same ones) granted Almodóvar the insight and perception of a cinematic master. Even those in Spain and Britain who had previously been sceptical of Almodóvar's achievement (such as Angel Fernández-Santos and Alexander Walker) were won over by his tour de force, momentarily allowing sentiment to suffuse their critical faculties. They were thus willing to overlook the extreme heterogeneity of the narrative, a characteristic they had previously attacked. Intermittently interrupted by apparently incongruous elements (two dance pieces by Pina Bausch, a set piece song by Caetano Veloso, an eight minute recreation of a silent film in luscious black and white) the film as a whole is unified by formal elements that are purely cinematic.

This is once more a link with Nussbaum, whose intelligent emotions need not be linguistic or verbal: cognition is not to be reduced to "calculation, computation, or reflexive self-awareness," but is rather simply "receiving and processing information" (2001, 23). Indeed the "cognitive structure of compassion" (*ibid.*, 304) is experienced through transitional objects ("through symbolic activity the child cultivates her ability to imagine what others experience" [*ibid.*, 238]) and through music. Beyond Almodóvar's typically wordy dialogue, then, heightened mise en scène and soundtrack serve to educate the spectator and listener into new structures of feeling whose values and associations are difficult to delimit. As ever, Almodóvar exploits colour to taint our perceptions, idiosyncratically painting the walls of the clinic in warm orange and olive. Moreover objects migrate from hand to hand and place to place, bearing a passional charge with them. Most nomadic (and enigmatic) is the hair grip stolen by Benigno from Alicia's bedroom, given by him in prison to Marco, and returned by the latter to Benigno's grave. The sensitive US website, by distributor Sony Classics, paintshops clickable props into the hushed, hermetic room in which Benigno stands suspended in the light of the window (Sony). He is represented by the hair grip, the mobile Marco by his cell phone, and Lydia by a framed photo of the corrida. Alicia is imaged in the lava lamp which will join her in hospital and whose red pulse, suddenly swollen to the full size of the cinema screen, will stand in for the rape and insemination which we are not allowed to witness.

Music occupies a similar supplementary role in the film, at once standing in for something that is absent and outstripping something that is present. Alberto Iglesias's fourth soundtrack for Almodóvar is typically expert, but newly prominent. The suite for the silent *El amante menguante* (*The Shrinking Lover*) is a self-conscious pastiche that displaces both dialogue within the interpolated narrative and action outside it. Specialist site Film Music on the Web notes how the suite's "strong solo on cello" is taken up later by a "lovely piano solo" on *Alicia vive* (*Alicia Lives*). Even the titles given by Iglesias to his often brief "cues" (titles that are of course denied to theatrical audiences) hint at meanings unspecified at a plot level: for example, *Sábana santa* (*Holy Sheet*) points to the injured purity of Alicia (actress Leonor Watling's fan website is similarly known as *La princesa herida* [*The Wounded Princess*]). "Source cues" (i.e. pre-existing musical fragments) also suggest an amorous knowledge irreducible to calculation or computation. Caetano's melancholic cooing transforms a hackneyed folk song; Purcell's "Plaint: O Let Me Weep" from *The Faerie Queen*, which a Spanish audience would be hard pressed to identify, subtly reinforces Marco's tears. Indeed by beginning with an uncompromisingly abstract dance piece, Almodóvar is suggesting that the meaning of his film cannot be reduced to rational discourse, that the "eloquence of the body" (his phrase) must take precedence in aesthetics as in ethics. If cinema (like the much mourned lost object) "takes up residence in the lives of the speaker and listener" (also Almodóvar's words), then that inhabitation or cohabitation is disturbingly volatile. Nussbaum puts it in almost identical terms: "Past loves shadow present attachments and take up residence within them" (2001, 2).

Of course it is this question of compassion or the "willingness to live in interdependence with others" (Nussbaum 2001, 13) that has provoked most controversy amongst viewers. Benigno's rape is hardly consistent with Nussbaum's "reform" of love. Needy, vengeful, and partial, Benigno has no respect for reciprocity or individuality. Yet presented as his passion is in a social and psychological context, we are tempted nonetheless to understand him intuitively. And once more mise en scène argues for an unconscious and generous identification that transcends intellectual detachment: when Marco visits Benigno in prison their two faces, reflected in the endless glass walls of the cubicles, are fused into one (Figure 2). It is an effect that Almodóvar claims was accidental. It is appropriate however for a film which one Spanish critic, invoking San Juan de la Cruz, called "una lucha de la inteligencia amorosa con el misterio que le rodea y que la razón no puede comprender" ("A struggle of amorous intelligence with the mystery which surrounds it and which reason cannot understand") (De verdad). Given their specific circumstances, we should remain with Nussbaum suspicious of the content of Benigno's feelings. We cannot, however, discount their childhood history (clearly displayed to us) and their unpredictable and disorderly operation in the daily life of "human beings who are attached to things outside themselves" (Nussbaum 2001, 2).

If Almodóvar's broad ethical argument is perfectly accessible to spectators of different nationalities in spite of its imagistic expression, then the precise social implications of his amorous intelligence are more elusive. In accordance with recent changes in the constitution of the cinema audience which have in Spain (as in Mexico) rendered moviegoing a relatively elite activity, Almodóvar's madrileños inhabit a privileged, urban environment in which, as in Woody Allen's New York, a comfortable income is simply taken for granted: there can be few nurses in Madrid who enjoy Benigno's freedom to redecorate his apartment on a whim after seeing a layout in a glossy magazine. Hermetic and self-referential, the Almodóvar "universe" has become immune to social stresses. Even such particularizing elements as Lydia's Andalusian family are curiously unfocused: Ana Fernández as the sister, brilliant as the bruised and abused daughter in Benito Zambrano's Solas, is sadly wasted in Hable, lost amongst the folkloric candles and medals. A film such as Hable, however, remains an "event movie" for audiences in Spain, most especially after the unusually long delay that followed Todo sobre mi madre (All About My Mother). Unlike a Hollywood movie, Hable is consciously chosen by Spanish audiences on the basis of the director's renown. Admission figures show that Almodóvar's shift upmarket has not cost him a mass audience (albeit one reconfigured in the way I mentioned earlier): the film grossed almost a million dollars in its opening weekend on an unprecedented 276 Spanish screens (Green 2002). But unlike television drama, the unique event of the feature film need not fight to be seen and heard amongst the messy and disorderly operations of everyday life. Quality television drama that manages to do so thus requires particular respect and attention.

Cuéntame cómo pasó: the emotional history of objects

There is no doubting the centrality of television to domestic life in Spain. In *Políticas de televisión*, a recent academic survey of the "configuration of the audiovisual market," Eduardo Giordano and Carlos Zeller (1999) stress the reconfiguration of intrafamilial communication which accompanied the "irruption" of TV: "transformando el tradicional esquema espacial (centrípeto) de 'mesa redonda' por otro (centrífugo de 'semicírculo abierto'), con un vértice que imanta la atención del grupo hacia el televisor" ("transforming the traditional (centripetal) spatial format of the 'round table' with another centrifugal format (of the 'open semi-circle') (*ibid.*, 21). Interestingly, however, the authors reject the commonplace assumption of another "invasion," that of US cultural imperialism. Rather, they say, this has been used as an "alibi" to avoid thinking more creatively about European culture (*ibid.*, 53). The progressive degradation of state-controlled TVE in the 1990s is an example of this creative exhaustion. Giving up on the ideal of "public service," TVE copied the new private channels, seeking mass audiences and filling newly extended hours of broadcasting with imports and TV movies (including Latin American telenovelas).

Lorenzo Díaz's (1999) report on what he calls "the abominable decade" of the 1990s stresses rather the historical memory of Spanish viewers. Thus the 1960s saw not only the notorious "age of prizes" (including Massiel's famous triumph for Spain in the Eurovision Song Contest), but also the "mester de progresía" ("politically liberal creativity") in which budding cineastes such as Josefa Molina and Jaime Chávarri brought high culture to the unsuspecting masses (1999, 55–6). Public television was then noted for "quality series drama," with Molina adapting such authors as Ibsen and even Proust (*ibid.*, 83). Now the public is polarized with the high and middle brow preferences of the modern, Europeanized audience overwhelmed by the tastes of "la España profunda" ("traditionalist Spain"): Lina Morgan, much loved clown of 1960s film farce, remained prime time TV queen in the late 1990s (*ibid.*, 99).

Ironically enough "quality" programming (Díaz cites *The X Files* and *The Simpsons*) is more likely to come from the once despised USA (*ibid.*, 175). It seems Spanish television deserves the half-hearted attention it attracts from spectators: 61.4% of the population turn on the TV "out of habit" and a similar number "always have dinner" with the TV on (*ibid.*, 213–14).

Both surveys were completed just before the explosion of domestically produced quality series that I have studied elsewhere (Smith 2003). Indeed even Díaz notes the long time popularity on the small screen of such skilled film actors as Imanol Arias and Ana Belén. While workplace dramas such as *Periodistas* ("Journalists") were pioneered by private web Tele 5 (Smith 2003, 16–24), public TVE fought back with domestic period drama *Cuéntame*, now in its third year the most popular programme in Spain. *Cuéntame* has repeatedly won prizes, both domestic and foreign: even Bulgarian audiences, who emerged more recently than Spaniards from dictatorship, have taken the series to heart. Like Almodóvar's recent feature films, then, it is a rare case in the Spanish audiovisual market where mass audience and critical acclaim coincide.

As is well known, television (unlike cinema) is charged with providing information as well as entertainment. And the emotional pleasures of series drama, more or less coextensive with those of everyday life, are repeatedly qualified by the supposed educational content of this show. Set in the late 1960s, it follows the fortunes of the middle class Alcántara family: father Antonio (played by Imanol Arias), mother Mercedes (Ana Duato), and their three children, teenagers Toni and Ines and infant Carlos, whose grown up alter ego provides a syrupy voice over. Able support is given by the grandmother, played by María Galiana (unforgettable as the abused wife and mother in *Solas*). Produced by an independent company (Grupo Ganga) and with a high budget that permits frequent location shots (a convincingly grey and grimy Alcalá de Henares substitutes for Madrid) and the seamless insertion of fictional characters into authentic period documentary (No-Do newsreel is a constant reference). Spanish viewers do not seem disconcerted by the acknowledged influence here of US nostalgia fests *The Wonder Years* and *Forrest Gump*. The programme also prides itself on the authenticity of its studio-shot interiors, crammed with original artefacts. *Cuéntame*'s casting, cinematography, and art design thus combine to reinforce an impression of "quality" still relatively rare on Spanish television, helping the show to distinguish itself from the messy domestic disorder in which typically it is consumed.

Ironically, however, unlike Tele 5's workplace dramas that focus on professional life, *Cuéntame* is consistently directed to the home. Indeed it calls attention to the centrality of television to emotional history in Spain: the publicity still that graces the soundtrack CD (music is vital to the show's sentimental appeal) shows the family grouped around their period TV set and the cast frequently watch television (Figure 3). Often meal shots reveal the regular characters enacting the change in family communication effected by television: they sit around three sides of the table with the father facing the camera, where the new television is also placed.

Cuéntame has been seen as part of a new interest in historical memory enacted by such diverse cultural phenomena as the recent exhibition on the Spanish exile community and the continued search for war burial sites ("Remembering"). Indeed the documentary *El exilio* (*Exile*) was also carried by TVE, albeit on its minority second channel. However, the somewhat hermetic reflexivity of the show (with the on-screen period family directly mirroring their off-screen present day counterparts) and the warm emotionalism of the narratives seem to have taken the edge off the avowed educational or informational intent. Even viewers active enough to post their opinions in an internet chatroom are hazy as to the period represented, which they cite variously and erroneously as "the 1950s" or "twenty years ago" (dooyoo). While some critics praise the informational value of the programme, claiming alternately and paradoxically either that it shows the pains of dictatorship or that it shows the pleasures of a preconsumerist era, viewers focus rather on the production design. Calling the series a "museum of memory," listings magazine *Tele Indiscreta* offer a list of emotionally resonant commodities: "la máquina de coser, el tresillo de skay, el pick up y el 850" ("the sewing machine, the leatherette couch, the record player and 850 [cheap make of car]") ('Museo').

There is no doubt that *Cuéntame*, for all its awards, privileges the emotional over the social or political. Typically the polished plots undercut adult concerns through ironic parallels with the children. Thus the father's *amiguetes* (cronies), fretting over money at the bar, are contrasted with the child's little friends, arguing over the Reyes

Magos in the street. Teenage Toni's political commitment is shown to be dependent on his love for a radical student. His gift of a banned book by Wilhelm Reich is an attempt at an education that is purely sentimental (he, unlike his cool comrade, is ignorant of the work's contents). This special episode for the holiday, broadcast on 10 January 2002, compares the secret wishes of each family member: the married couple long for a romantic weekend in a hotel; the tearful teenager for "immaterial things" (the reciprocation of his love for the revolutionary student); little Carlos cannot bear to choose between a Fort Apache and a Scalextrix racing set (we are treated to period commercials for these long lost products in the opening sequence). In the previous episode, which coincided with Christmas, the adults' obsession with the lottery is subverted by the children's improvised raffle, boasting such prizes as Agustina de Aragón's brassiere, Tarzan's toilet paper, and the fork which once belonged to El Cid Campeador. The burlesquing of history is transparent. Even when serious issues are addressed the focus is on mise en scène. When Inés's friend confesses to the worker priest (another period stereotype) that she is pregnant a life size statue of the Virgin is set between her and the camera. In the same episode our view of father and son is obstructed by a much desired new printing press and the whole family is shot from behind the television, now the focal point of a domestic drama which had begun with a closeup of a large, wall mounted radio set.

Cuéntame appeals too frequently to hindsight, gently flattering the modern democratic and consumerist audience: Toni inscribes his gift "in a time when buying books was forbidden;" lost in a snow-drift on the sierra, Antonio longs for a time when mobile phones are a possibility. What I would argue, however, is that in spite of these conceptual or intentional shortcomings the series engages in a non-linguistic amorous intelligence or emotional cognition which (as in Almodóvar) transcends plot and dialogue. Like Nussbaum's Proust, Cuéntame traces the "history [of the emotions] in infancy and child-hood" and invokes a "cognitive structure that is narrative in form, involving a story of our relation to cherished objects that extends over time" (Nussbaum 2001, 2).

The co-extensiveness of fictional time with calendar time (albeit skewed by the requirements of the TV "season") reinforces this tem-poral charge. The emotional profile of the actors (invisible to foreigners who know them only from film) is vital here too. Arias and Duato are known in the press as Spain's "most stable married couple," having previously played man and wife in a miniseries on Nobel Prize winner Severo Ochoa. Ana Belén, the quintessential progre woman of the period, is joined on the title song by her son, in another instance of emotional thickening or enrichening. Like Almodóvar's lava lamp and hair grip, the props on which such loving attention is lavished in Cuéntame cannot simply suggest a facile nostalgia that could hardly account for the appeal of the show to its huge audience. They also take on the privileged quality of emotional objects, which according to Nussbaum are not intentional but rather embody ways of seeing, beliefs, and the attribution of values (2001, 28).

Antonio gives his novelty obsessed and ungrateful son the old fashioned watch that his own father had given him on his deathbed. All of Cuéntame's art design is haloed by this unrecognised, anticipated mourning, which can only be understood when we (when the child) have grown into that present position from which we watch the show. There is, as Nussbaum puts it, a "double aspect of loss" here: "it alludes to the value of the person who has left or died, but it alludes as well to that person's relation to the perspective of the mourner" (2001, 31). Careless or heedless Spanish audiences may well be unable to identify the historical period in which Cuéntame is set. But they can hardly avoid (indeed clearly respond intensely to) the "ladder of love" it proposes. The latter leads from the most banal of everyday objects to the most precious of human relationships, invisibly enhanced by the anticipation of loss. As in Proust's magic lantern once more, the room the audience is actually in is coloured with or illuminated by the images of other stories.

Audiovisual ambivalence

In a press release of November 2002 TVE proudly trumpeted an increasing lead over its rivals (with a share of 24%), which was due in part to Spain's top-rated drama: Cuéntame had beaten its own record with 6,874,000 viewers and a 39.6% share (TVE). The same release noted that average daily viewing time had risen to 227 minutes, twelve minutes up on the previous month and two minutes on the same month of the previous year. In this context of consumption, cinema is increasingly dependent on television. Moreover the film industry is newly worried by a merger between two rival pay TV platforms (Green 'Film Industry'). It is feared that this will threaten local production by forcing down presale prices of feature films to television.

A treasured object to many Spaniards, television is also ambivalent, inspiring as much rage as love. As shown by their reactions on websites such as dooyoo, some viewers clearly fear even a fiction as apparently benign as *Cuéntame*. The ambivalence of the relation to the past was also taken up by Almodóvar. In a moving piece on his attendance at the funeral of pop musician Carlos García Berlanga, the director refers nostalgically to time past or lost: "aquellos maravillosos años, que se han dado en llamar 'la movida'" ("those wonderful years which have come to be called 'the movida'") (Almodóvar 2002). But retrospection is, as ever, tinged by regret: Pedro and Carlos's generation were "descarada, atrevida, frívola e inconoclasta, pero terriblemente tímida" ("shameless, daring, frivolous, and iconoclastic, but terribly shy"). Berlanga spent his last days in the same clinic where Almodóvar had shot *Hable*; and, all unknowing, the director unfurls the same umbrella at the cemetery that he had used for the scene of the son's death in *Todo sobre mi madre*. Once more culture is a model for a lesson in amorous intelligence, shaping the geography of emotional life.

Almodóvar mourns the movida, as *Cuéntame* commemorates the more problematic period of the 1960s. If we read both as emotional imperatives, however, they can be seen as an elusive "education for compassionate citizenship" (Nussbaum 2001, 432) that is irreducible to conscious control or linguistic means. This has gender implications also. For as Nussbaum reminds us, if the moral and sentimental education of women is more socially cultivated, it is because they still suffer greater vulnerability and helplessness in the face of objects they cannot control (*ibid.*, 376–7). Both works feminize men: *Hable*'s Marco weeps from the opening scene; *Cuéntame*'s father is helplessly lost in the snow and, in a unique breach in the realist mise en scène, is rescued by a modernized version of the Three Kings, ethnically diverse drivers of a monster truck from the twenty-first century. Nussbaum writes: "Emotions are thus, in effect, acknowledgements of neediness and lack of self-sufficiency" (*ibid.*,

22). Taking up residence within us, these Spanish audiovisual fictions also remind us of the importance of external objects to our own flourishing. This is the final moral, at once ethical and aesthetic, of the emotional imperative.

Works cited

Almodóvar, Pedro. 'Crónica de un adiós.' *El País* [Madrid] 16 June 2002, 34.

Díaz, Lorenzo. *Informe sobre la televisión en España*. Barcelona: Ediciones B, 1999.

Fernández-Santos, Angel. 'Viaje más allá de la soledad y la muerte' [review of *Hable con ella*]. *El País* [Madrid] 15 March 2002, 40.

Giordano, Eduardo and Zeller, Carlos. *Políticas de televisión*. Barcelona: Icaria, 1999.

Green, Jennifer. '*Talk to Her (Hable con ella)*' [review]. *Screen International* 22 March 2002, 18.

Nussbaum, Martha C. *Upheavals of Thought: The Intelligence of Emotions*. Cambridge: Cambridge University Press, 2001.

Smith, Paul Julian. *Desire Unlimited: The Cinema of Pedro Almodóvar*. First edition. London and New York: Verso, 1994.

—. *Desire Unlimited: The Cinema of Pedro Almodóvar*. Second edition. London and New York: Verso, 2002.

—. *Contemporary Spanish Culture: TV, Fashion, Art, and Film*. Oxford and Cambridge: Polity, 2003.

Walker, Alexander. 'The Spanish connection' [review of *Hable con ella*]. *Evening Standard* [London] 22 August 2002, 51.

Electronic sources

Almodóvar, Pedro. Official Spanish website of *Hable con ella*. Accessed 2 September 2003 www.clubcultura.com/clubcine/clubcineastas/almodovar/hableconella/sinopsis.htm

De verdad. '*Hable con ella* de Pedro Almodóvar.' [review] 2 May 2002. Accessed 11 July 2002 www.uce.es/DEVERDAD/ARCHIVO_2002/05_02/DV05_02_19hableconella.html

dooyoo. Consumer Product Review website. Chat room on *Cuéntame*. Accessed 6 December 2002. www.dooyoo.es/product/270468.html

Film Music on the Web. Soundtrack review of *Hable con ella*. 2 May
2002. Accessed 11 July 2002. www.musicweb.uk.net/film/
2002/May02/Hable_con_Ella.html

Green, Jennifer. 'Film industry worries over Spanish pay-tv
merger.' *Screen Daily* 6 December 2002. www.screendaily.com

Princesa Herida. Unofficial website of actress Leonor Watling.
Accessed 11 July 2002. www.princesaherida.com

Sony. Official US webite. Accessed 6 December 2002.
www.sonyclassics.com/talktoher

teleindiscreta. 'Memoria de otra época.' Article on *Cuéntame*.
24 December 2001. Accessed 6 December 2002.
www.teleindiscreta.navegalia.com

—. 'Museo para la memoria.' Article on *Cuéntame*. 3 June 2002.
Accessed 6 December 2002.

TVE. 'Audiencias Noviembre 2002.' *TVE Informa Revista de Prensa*
9 December 2002. www.rtve.es

Family plots: the politics of affect in Spanish television drama of the millennium

2

Passion and television

Luisa Passerini is a feminist oral historian who has studied such varied topics as the generation of 1968 in Italy, the history of working-class movements and Fascism, and the idea of love in Europe, and more particularly, in Britain between the world wars (Passerini 1987, 1996, 1999). In spite of the diversity of these themes (and the range of sources studied), Passerini's work forms a distinctive and challenging body with a guiding thread throughout: the interconnection of ideas, feelings, and relations in cultural identity. Exploring the lost connections between love, culture, and ideology, Passerini's argument is broadly that rational choices, supposedly objective, cannot be separated from emotional choices. In keeping with this revaluation of subjectivity, she has on occasion bravely incorporated her own autobiography and psychoanalysis into her chronicles of affect. Engaging with the thorny and hoary problem of feminine identity (or 'Becoming a subject in the time of the death of the subject'), Passerini combines self-reflection or self-imaging with a self-irony, using humour to dedramatize narcissism.

When studying the oral memory of Fascism in Turin's working class, Passerini noted the way in which informants often omitted altogether the most dramatic or traumatic elements of national political history. She read this omission or repression both negatively as testimony to "wounds" as yet unhealed and positively as a tribute to the preoccupations of everyday life which were valued even in the most disruptive circumstances (quoted in Popular Memory Group). These iconic or shareable life stories are thus practical examples of a theoretical preoccupation: the restitution of subjectivity, and most especially female subjectivity, on the level of interpretation (Passerini 1991, 8). The practice of oral history leads to the possibility of a privileged "transmission:"

The mutual recognition of self and other [*altra*] in the full sense of the communicative relation even amongst unequals, between mother and daughter, teacher and pupil [*maestra e allieva*], between different generations, in the affects and the intellect. (1991, 11)

Interestingly it is the existence of this "disparity" (typical of both the mother and the teacher) which Passerini stresses as the source of the "joy and surprise" of a successful transmission which takes place in conditions of freedom (1991, 12).

Passerini presents the more recent implications of her project most clearly in an article with Elena Pulcini: "European feminine identity and the idea of passion in politics" (Passerini and Pulcini 2002). Here two clusters of concepts are brought together: identity and love, and passion and love and Europe. The authors reject the familiar feminist critique of "women, passion, and the compulsory bond of affectivity" (*ibid.*, 98). They argue that "private is no longer a synonym for privation or deprivation," after the "radical transformation of the image of the family in the light of modern individualism" and the "new affective code" of love marriages and the quest for personal happiness (*ibid.*, 100). Love cannot be dismissed as a "screen for inequality" (*ibid.*, 101). It may be the case that post-Enlightenment Europe "builds an image of woman as the subject of sentiment" while depriving her of two fundamental rights: "the right of citizenship and the right of passion ... of excess, disorder, conflict" (*ibid.*, 101). But the feminist project as they see it is:

[The] revaluation of the link between woman and affectivity ... not a segregation of woman to the closed and sweetened world of affections, but an appreciation of the peculiarity of the female subject to reconcile freedom and dependence, rationality and affectivity, autonomy and responsibility ... . (*ibid.*, 102)

Passerini and Pulcini are, of course, fully aware of the possibility of being branded "essentialists" here. But as historians they seek rather an "emotional basis [for] the idea of Europe ... linked to an active memory of emotions" (*ibid.*, 107), even as they remain suspicious of the "conformist marital love in modern times [and] the massification of culture represented by popular fiction and television culture" (*ibid.*, 108).

One methodological innovation of Passerini is the rejection of the distinction between primary sources and secondary references (1999, 319). This is in line with the extreme diversity of material she treats: oral testimony, manuscript archives (love letters), and printed texts of all kinds (from romantic novels to theological treatises). I am struck, however, by the dismissive reference to television in the one essay. While TV raises the same question as the oral history interview (monologue or dialogue?), it is surely another test case for the revaluation of the domestic and everyday. Indeed it stages more clearly than some of Passerini's textual sources that interrelation between public and private life which we might call the affective politics of the nation.

In this chapter I address two recent Spanish TV dramas that revolve around very different definitions of the family and the private sphere. *Médico de familia* (*Family Doctor*) was the phenomenon of Spanish television over the period 1995–99. The highest rated and best loved series drama of the period, it made star and producer Emilio Aragón the ubiquitous and unchallenged king of Spanish entertainment (he even appeared on a postage stamp). While previously I have attacked *Médico de familia* for being (unlike the workplace dramas which superseded it) "unapologetically domestic and everyday" (Smith 2003, 28), I now believe it can be reread as a history of Spanish sentiments (most especially that vague but valuable quality of "simpatía"). A notoriously sunny show, it is in fact strangely shadowed by social issues, which force their way into the extended family's suburban haven. Moreover as the saviour of new private web Tele 5 (part owned by Silvio Berlusconi) and as an original format exported to many other countries, *Médico de familia* raises vital questions of "national culture," i.e. the congruence of the frontiers of states and those of cultural communities (Collins 1991). This is not to suggest that Spain is inherently "emotional" as compared to other countries, thus confirming a long held stereotype. It is rather to propose that there are distinctive national regimes of affect which can be glimpsed in genres, such as TV drama, that are often dismissed or despised for their supposed sentimentality.

Cultural sovereignty or the maintenance of a national culture is also raised by my second example, *7 Vidas* (literally *Seven Lives*, figuratively *Nine Lives*), the most profitable scripted show since it began its first season on Tele 5 in 1999. An innovator both industrially and generically, like *Médico de familia*, *7 Vidas* claims to be the first Spanish sitcom produced according to US production processes. Yet, as we shall see, it is unusually explicit and precise in its references to Spanish politics, addressing parliamentary concerns deliberately neglected by both *Médico de familia* and its spokesman Aragón. Moreover *7 Vidas*' family could not be further from *Médico de familia*'s traditionalist suburbanites. A de facto rather than de jure community (in Spanish "de hecho," not "de derecho"), *7 Vidas*' urban companions form an elective family that is conspicuously urban and contemporary. Suspiciously close to the template of the six *Friends*, the seven or eight shifting protagonists of Tele 5's sitcom embrace a wider range of generations, political allegiances, and sexual preferences than the New York-set original. For example, the regular characters include a lesbian actress and a Communist retiree. The discontinuity between the two Tele 5 shows thus raises problems of both corporate mentality (how can the same company produce such diverse content?) and national culture (how can the same audience tolerate such sudden and radical shifts in sensibility and morality?). Family plots that are related, if not twinned, *Médico de familia* and *7 Vidas* stage politics of affect that will prove to have more in common than might be expected at first sight.

Médico de familia: a sentimental transmission

The premise of *Médico de familia*, the "mother of new Spanish series drama" (Todotv), is given as follows by Emilio Aragón's own production company, Globomedia:

El joven médico [Nacho Martín] tiene tres hijos [María, Chechu, Anita] y un sobrino adolescente a su cargo. La serie, contada en clave comico-dramática, cuenta los problemas familiares, personales, y profesionales que le acucian, que son los que interesan y afectan a todos los humanos. Pero no está solo, vive con su padre [Manolo] y la asistenta de la casa [Juani], que marcan el ritmo diario de la vida familiar (Muchatv)

A young doctor [Nacho Martín] has three children [María, Chechu, Anita] and a teenage nephew in his care. The series, which is told in a semi-comic manner, narrates the family, personal, and professional problems which concern him, problems which interest and affect all human beings. But he is not alone, as he lives with his father [Manolo] and the housekeeper [Juani], who mark out the daily rhythm of family life.

It is clear from this synopsis that the focus is not on Nacho's workplace, a reassuringly antiseptic and irreproachably modern health centre, but on his extended, indeed constantly expanding, domestic ménage. Although exteriors show the home to be in a Spanish version of the suburbs (tall but narrow terraced houses, fronted by tiny gardens), the interiors of the kitchen and living room suggest a US-style ranch house, with ample horizontal space. The aim of the production design seems to be to give an impression of comfortable domesticity, intended to stimulate the aspirations, both affective and economic, of an audience whose families were now reduced to small nuclear units and for whom a live-in housekeeper was at best a distant memory. The numerous Martín family (supplemented in the last seasons by Nacho's new wife and twins) lounge on well stuffed, colourful sofas or congregate around the kitchen table where breakfast is served by big-hearted, loud-mouthed Andalusian Juani to as many as a dozen characters of at least three different generations (Figure 4). A print by Chagall on the stairs signals professional status, while Nacho's Lacoste polo shirts suggest quiet good taste, inattentive to the whims of fashion.

Looking back on the show, current websites stress its lack of "quality" in spite of its importance for the history of Spanish TV (Muchatv); or criticize its "moralizing" and "insipid" view of a Spain invisible "out in the street" (Paramountcomedy). In spite of its attempts to address social issues, *Médico de familia* suffers from "an overdose of good intentions" ("buenos sentimientos"). Nacho Martín, the character of Emilio Aragón (who receives a credit as composer as well as executive producer) is frequently described as "simpático." It is an ill defined but vital affective quality reinforced by the career profile of the actor himself, who first appeared on television as a circus clown, and worked his way up through game and variety shows. Typically, Aragón won an award as the most "loved" host of the latter (Urjc).

Aragón, whose huge popularity remains something of a mystery to this foreign viewer, is thus an exemplary case of that paradoxical combination of the ordinary and the exceptional which is thought to be typical of stars. Lanky and toothy, he keeps his glasses on even in the shower (typically, he is surprised by intrusive workmen when he moves into the new family home). Neither too handsome nor too young, he is the perfect *novio de España* ("Spain's boyfriend" or "fiancé"). The term is significant, because what Nacho lacks is a wife: she has died in a car accident one year before the series begins. If, as Globomedia knowingly wrote in its publicity material, *Médico de familia* combines familial, personal, and professional elements, it is the personal which will give the series its longevity, based on a long running plot strand of unresolved sexual tension between Nacho and Alicia (Lydia Bosch), his journalist sister-in-law. While Nacho is good-hearted but shy (too timid to confess his feelings to Alicia), she is (according to the character profiles) "independent [but] nervous and tremendously jealous" (Paramountcomedy). If *Médico de familia* is conformist and insipid, typical of those massified hymns to domesticity so common in television culture, it is founded nonetheless on a wound (the absent mother) which will remain unhealed as long as the writers continue to place obstacles in the path of the principals' true love.

Médico de familia's hermetic universe, shot almost exclusively on set in the first seasons, might seem to exemplify Passerini's romantic segregation: a closed and sweetened world of affections. Yet the absence of the mother means that this realm is not exclusively identified with women. The ineffectual Nacho (who, to take three plot points from different episodes, is unable to fix the electricity, use a computer, or ski) is clearly feminized, as both the main subject and object of love. Even when wearing his white coat he seems more a friendly counsellor than a respected physician. Invariably his professional issues are reframed in personal terms that often leave him at a loss. For example, his inability to master computer software enables a female colleague whose advances he has rejected to impose a schedule which requires him to be on duty during the holiday season. The series thus stages an ambivalent schooling in sentiment for men from one generation to another: the child Chechu is told he should not cry by a grandfather who is later in tears himself; Nacho, caught between the generations, is taught lessons in love by everyone.

The production history of the show, documented by *El Mundo*, confirms that this shareable narrative is riven by unacknowledged conflict (Aragón and Sánchez Navas 1997). A set report celebrates the "familiarity" and "positivity" of the atmosphere after episode 64 had achieved an extraordinary rating of 9.5 millions and a share of 51%. But the secret of the show's success is its self-conscious address to different and mutually exclusive demographics: middle-aged, middle-class women admire professional Alicia; the working-class Juani and electrician Poli pull in the lower paid; grandfather Manolo procures the elderly; while children and teenagers tune in (even for a show that begins at 10pm) thanks to Nacho's three children and nephew. The trick, writes the journalist, is not so much to please everyone as to "not displease anyone."

Carefully calibrated as "family entertainment," *Médico de familia*, according to Aragón himself, benefits from a flexible production system through which "the product adapts to the tastes of the audience as the latter changes" (Aragón and Sánchez Navas 1997). New actors and characters are thus incorporated in order to fill gaps in the audience profile. As the original child actors age in "real time," there is a "parallelism" between them and the viewers which increases the potency of the series' identification and complicity to an audience that has grown accustomed to its "rhythm." But this knowing exploitation of national sentiment, in all its diversity and particularity, is inseparable from social issues. Themes of this kind, which are also an indispensable feature of the show, are chosen for their suitability for the *sobremesa* (after-meal discussion) in Spanish family homes. This "solidarity" is quite literally incorporated into the show: Nacho's fictional clinic is dressed with posters from real charities fighting alcoholism or promoting awareness of diabetes sent in by concerned viewers. To its credit, *Médico de familia* also gave a substantial role in its final season to an actor with Down's syndrome.

This meticulous process of production and promotion, unprecedented in Spain, is an unexpected and to some unwelcome example of the fusion of rational and emotional choices which Passerini advocates in the very different context of oral history. But if the professional is personalized in the series (the computerization of the workplace reduced to a lovers' tiff), then the emotional is also socialized (expressed in terms of broadly political implication). Thus while Manolo lives with his son's family, one episode features mistreatment of the elderly in retirement homes. Identities, feelings, and relations flow across boundaries of age and gender. The grandfather says he is permitted to cry, but only because he is no longer a man; teenage María is asked to take on the role of mother, which is also filled intermittently and problematically by ambitious Alicia and overworked Nacho. By later episodes Juani has established an extended ménage of her own with workmen Poli and Marcial, the proletarian mirror image of the bourgeois Martíns. Class divisions are masked, but return as conflicts of taste: the family roundly ridicules the frilly pink lamps Juani buys as a wedding gift for her employer (she substitutes a more sober night stand in handsome wood). *Médico de familia* is thus an unlikely but efficient agent for a schooling not just in emotion but in what Bourdieu (1984) calls the social production of aesthetics. The 43.2% of the working class that watched the show (Aragón and Sánchez Navas 1997) no doubt took note of Juani's shame and confusion over the inappropriate gift.

But just as networks track the ratings of their shows as they fluctuate from minute to minute, so the passionate politics of television makes sense only on closer examination. Let us look at three specimen episodes. The first episode was screened on 12 September 1995 and directed by Daniel Ecija (later to produce *Periodistas* and *7 Vidas*). The precredit sequence introduces the large cast through the viewfinder of child Chechu's camcorder, while the credits themselves show pseudo-family snapshots of Nacho and wife before his bereavement. The episode narrates a move from an apartment in the city centre to the new suburbs. It is surprising how explicit the script is on the relation between personal and spatial practices. A running gag says that if you want to do anything (from buying chewing gum to seeing friends) you have to go to the mall. When Nacho praises the unaccustomed trees, his teenage daughter says they will be great to hang yourself from. She also suggests that housekeeper Juani will not be allowed into the new suburb without a passport. Lengthening his commute, the new house makes Nacho late for work. His first case is a pregnant schoolgirl. The miniskirted nurse notes tartly that it is easy enough for doctors "who live in *chalets* [country houses]" and know nothing of unemployment to counsel against abortion (in fact, Nacho has rigorously reserved judgement). The authority of father and physician is thus gently but consistently undermined, and objective and reasonable ideas (of a better neighbourhood, a more informed choice) are qualified by subjective and unruly emotions (homesickness, envy).

By the end of the episode (just over an hour of footage, stretched to almost two hours by Tele 5's extended commercial breaks) most of these plot points will be resolved: the girl keeps her baby (although aware that her chances of getting a boyfriend will now be remote); Nacho dances very badly to *bakalao* (Spanish electro) with his teenage daughter and her new suburban friend, a habituée of the mall. But the sentimental transmission across generations and genders remains open: Alicia advises Nacho on how to treat his growing daughter María (she has become a woman now that she buys her own underwear); but María comforts her aunt and substitute mother Alicia in her big city apartment when the latter has man trouble.

For the viewer, as for the screenwriters, subjectivity is thus incorporated at the level of interpretation: like Nacho, Alicia, and María we must listen with our heart as well as our head. This is yet clearer in a typical midseason episode (no. 14) which focuses on the long running theme of sexual tension. As in courtly love (a template mentioned by Pulcini and Passerini [2002, 104]), an emotional history is created through the placing of obstacles in the path of the protagonists. In this case both Nacho and Alicia have rival suitors (the computer-savvy doctor and a philandering journalist) and just when Nacho has plucked up the courage to confess his feelings Alicia announces that her boyfriend has asked her to marry him. Yet this is no mask for misogyny: both principals are exalted as objects of love, and each collapses on the either side of the door when the expected confession comes to nought. There is thus a sentimental symmetry in both scripting and "blocking" (the positioning of actors on the set).

This emotional climax is counterpointed, however, by one of the most explicitly political narratives in the series. María's gypsy classmate is to be withdrawn from school by her father. When the ever sympathetic Nacho visits the gypsy household (there is a brief establishing shot of *chabolas*), the patriarch angrily brushes them off, saying that *payos* (non-gypsies) do not understand the importance of family in gypsy culture and tradition. This is a contradiction which cannot be resolved, opposing as it does two basic features of the series: female autonomy and family loyalty. Indeed, Nacho admits as much in downbeat dialogue. The moral, he tells his daughter, is that you should do the right thing even if you fail. The gypsy girl is still excluded from the school (as she is from the narrative) and the limits of *Médico de familia*'s well meaning conformism exposed.

Comic relief is provided by the third narrative strand in which housekeeper Juani, unable to fit into a party dress, puts the whole family on a strict vegetarian diet. The centrality of food to a national culture is anxiously reaffirmed here. When the family finally throw out the greens, they sit down to the high fat and sugar comfort food of chocolate and *churros*. It is as if sentimental and social issues (unrequited love and education for minority women) can be assuaged only by the most primal of collective family activities: cooking. Grandfather Manolo makes the connection humorously explicit, saying: "I won't eat anything that didn't have a mother."

The inevitable wedding between Nacho and Alicia is postponed until episode 67 and is littered with comic obstacles until the very last moment. (Tele 5 even shot two versions of the ending, in one of which the wedding did not take place.) This event programming, which achieved an audience of 10,848,000 and a share of 60% in Christmas 1997 (Paramountcomedy), spares no expense, being shot almost entirely on location in the small town of Riaza, León. First, the priest is hospitalized, then Nacho is stuck in a snowstorm (we learn he is unable to ski) and is forced to get to the church by helicopter. Meanwhile the children have managed to stain Alicia's pristine dress with chocolate. Although, as I have mentioned, the Andalusians are mocked for their inappropriate present, Juani is inexplicably upgraded for the ceremony itself, swapping her *peineta* for a chic chignon and her folkloric skirt for a sleek black suit. At this emblematic moment, it is as if class conflict must be repressed even at the aesthetic level of taste. This cliffhanger episode (the last in the season) ends, however, with a literal grinding of gears: the airplane on which the newlyweds are flying on honeymoon makes a crash landing.

The last season features an even higher body count. Nacho swaps the safety of the studio-bound clinic for the drama (and costly exterior locations) of an ambulance. The final episodes showcase the bloody death of loveable Marcial (the electrician who had surprised Nacho in the shower four years earlier) and the lurid kidnapping of the youngest daughter by a deranged Santa Claus. It is an ambivalence far from the insipid unrealism and "good intentions" with which *Médico de familia* is now remembered. As Cosette Espindola de Castro (2003) writes in her excellent academic essay on the series, the "amorous discourse" of *Médico de familia* is generically and socially "hybrid." Just as *Médico de familia* fused elements of comedy of manners, melodrama, romance, and social drama, so it combined a central narrative leading to conformist conjugal love (itself shadowed by tragedy) with subplots featuring "latent" themes such as relationships of convenience or threesomes and separation. For Espindola the discourse of love which structures the show as a whole is itself contradictory, made up of three competing factors (intimacy, passion, and commitment) which are shown to be irreconcilable in any single relationship.

If *Médico de familia*'s plotting displayed curious contradictions which belie the smoothness of its address to its huge audience, then its achievement in scheduling terms was, as Espindola notes once more, to reformulate the relation of the Spanish family to television itself. With *Médico de familia* Tele 5, which was already preferred by women to the other networks, achieved a higher share than what were traditionally the uncontested and male oriented rating champions: international soccer games (Espindola 2003). The frontiers of the state and of the cultural community were thus reconformed in a feminine mode which provided the possibility at least for the recognition of same and other in a national sentimental history that was shareable by multiple and diverse groups.

7 Vidas: a politics of passionate irony

Espindola (2003) notes that the great absence from *Médico de familia* is sex. I would add humour, for those unamused by Juani's comic mock-Andalusianisms. Tele 5's groundbreaking sitcom *7 Vidas*, which premiered as *Médico de familia* was reaching the end of its run, focuses unerringly on these two themes. *7 Vidas* has shifted the boundaries of Spanish TV comedy by treating once taboo subjects and employing a smart and swift brand of wisecracking, reminiscent of US quality shows. It has thus attracted a smaller but more profitable demographic than *Médico de familia*'s anodyne but ambivalent family entertainment.

While the title *Médico de familia* suggests the coexistence and confusion of the personal and the professional (does the doctor treat the family or the family treat the doctor?), *7 Vidas* points simply to survival. Like the proverbial cat which features on its stylish logo, the show's characters always land on their feet. The theme of survival is characteristic of the show's highly urban environment. Although *7 Vidas* is videotaped live before a studio audience, scenes are linked by stock exteriors of anonymous and urgent urban life: pounding feet and surging traffic. And where *Médico de familia* was introduced by a saccharine instrumental, *7 Vidas*'s theme tune is a raw-throated rock number (which you can download to your cell phone from Tele 5's website). The difference is also clear from the sets. The main location of *7 Vidas* is a public space, the local bar called *Casi ke No* (the idiosyncratic spelling mirrors long time youth usage) (Figure 5). The bourgeois affluence of the Martíns is here exchanged for postmodern bric-a-brac. The walls are made of exposed brick and bright blue plaster, while the floors feature both tiles and stripped wood. The bar and stools are of perforated steel. On the walls hang a large still of Chaplin in *The Great Dictator* and (on the way to the toilet) a small print of Robert Indiana's famous LOVE print, with its lop-sided O. It is an interior which is knowingly unfinished and heterogeneous, displaying an urban sensibility that suggests both constant renovation and eclectic cosmopolitanism.

But *7 Vidas*' de facto family does not meet only in this public space. The second main location is the flat which Carlota, a middle aged hairstylist involved with bar owner Gonzalo, shares with other characters. In the 2003 season these are the younger on-off couple of Vero, who works in the music business, and feckless hippy-type Sergio. High up in an apartment building (a backdrop of the Madrid skyline is visible behind) the flat also boasts a shared terrace permitting sixty year old Sole, a Communist retiree, to drop in at inopportune moments. Carlota's home is, like the bar, an example of comfortable, but funky, urban chic: framed on the wall are Southeast Asian shadow puppets. As characters flow between the bar (which also contains an informal living space) and the two linked apartments they form new relations and express new sensations. The characters experience loneliness, abandonment, or unemployment in turn. Survival thus means improvising new forms of cohabitation which will prove both comic and conflictive. Privacy is no longer privation or deprivation here, but rather a valued if contested refuge from a problematic public sphere.

7 Vidas' credit sequence shows the regular cast being made up in their dressing rooms (mugging for the cameras) and making their entrance on to the sound stage through the cheering audience. It is an audacious and ironic beginning which chimes with the self-conscious sensibility of the well educated target audience. As the tenth season began in Spring 2003 (Spanish series, unlike their American equivalents, have at least two "seasons" a year), there was a lengthy feature on the show in *El País*, the quality newspaper which has long taken pride in dismissing television as trash. Stressing once more the survival of the series (which at four years and counting was now the longest running on Spanish television), the journalist gives a respectful account of the innovative production process (Sánchez-Mellado 2003). The chief executive producer, Nacho García Velilla, disappointed by established Spanish comedy writers, had flown to Hollywood to sit in on the making of *Frasier*. He then returned to Madrid to interview young untested hopefuls for the eleven person team of scriptwriters, who, as in the US, work in competition and collaboration with one another (*ibid.*, 58). The resulting characters and plot lines could not be further from those of "traditional series," with their "catalogue of professionals and impeccable parents and children" (*ibid.*, 58). And while *7 Vidas* does not achieve the ratings of earlier family viewing (gaining an average share of just 25%), its proportion of the most profitable "target" demographic (age 13–49, in cities of more than 100,000 inhabitants, middle-class and with higher education) rises to an exceptional 33% (*ibid.*, 59).

Although the journalist begins with a reference to *Friends* as a reference point and stresses the professionalism of *7 Vidas'* production process, she returns to national identity and domesticity as keys to the Spanish show's success. Jennifer Aniston, she claims, promotes expensive jewellery; her Spanish equivalents do spots for supermarkets. In spite of its cultural and even intellectual cachet, *7 Vidas* is familiar, even homely: "una serie de estar por casa. Donde mejor se está" ("A series where you feel at home. Which is where you feel best") (Sánchez-Mellado 2003, 59). Urban sophistication is thus undercut by a self-conscious irony which dedramatizes national narcissism.

This is a strategy prized by Passerini in her examination and promotion of feminine subjectivity. And it is clear that through laughter (for Passerini the royal road to both conscious and unconscious ["Becoming a Subject"]), *7 Vidas* attempts also to privilege a certain feminine subjectivity. In spite of high profile changes in the cast, with actors such as Javier Cámara leaving for prestigious film roles with the likes of Almodóvar, the main characters have remained predominantly female. Interestingly the actors all stress the "contradictory" nature of their roles. For Blanca Portillo, Carlota, self-sufficient but vulnerable, is "the modern woman, full of contradictions" (Sánchez-Mellado 2003, 54); Amparo Baró's Sole, the older Communist, is "no conventional granny [*abuelita*]" and would be incapable of playing bingo. Diana (Anabel Alonso), a B-list actress who recently came out of the closet, is the "craziest" in the series, but also the most courageous, fearless in defending her own lesbianism but shocked when her father has an affair (*ibid.*, 60). Gonzalo (Gonzalo de Castro), Carlota's intermittent partner, is explicitly feminized. The actor says his down in the mouth character is "very feminine," unsure how to cope with a woman who is a wild bull (*miura*) and torn between keeping up his reputation with male mates and not losing a woman he is crazy about. Like many couples today, says de Castro, Carlota and Gonzalo "make up their relationship from day to day" (*ibid.*, 61). The lesson in survival offered by *7 Vidas*, much more than the lesson in transmission given by the moralizing *Médico de familia*, is thus ambivalent and hard won.

Unlike *Médico de familia* which strove for a mass audience, *7 Vidas* is "TV for people who don't watch TV." And, also unlike its predecessor, it is performed by actors with no background in TV. In interview the cast stress their theatre credentials: Gonzalo de Castro was an assistant director at the Centro Dramático Nacional (Rodríguez 2003); Amparo Bardó trod the boards for thirty years and (like her character) was active in the trade union movement (Guadilla 2003); Carmen Machi, whose character is downtrodden cleaner Aída, had played Shakespeare on stage (López Monjas 2003). All of the actors praise the sophisticated humour of the series, so rare on Spanish television, and the multifaceted nature of the characters devised by the team written scripts.

As in *Médico de familia* once more, a central sentimental conflict (this time between Carlota and Gonzalo) is crosscut, albeit at a much faster pace, with social and historical references and, for the first time in Spanish TV comedy, party politics. Witty repartee interweaves these three areas, which are normally segregated. In one episode from 2001 (rerun on 2 April 2003), Sole berates her inattentive son visiting from Toledo: "Last time you came to see me coffee hadn't reached Europe;" he rejoins: "Last time you came to see me El Greco was still in art school." A snobby daughter-in-law is "a direct descendent of the Bourbons;" a baby nephew ("small, fat, and making strange noises") is compared to Catalan president Jordi Pujol. Actress Diana, who has decided to become a mother, is offered her dream job as she sits waiting at the sperm bank and must choose between parenthood and career. The personal, professional, and the political jostle for position in the quick-fire gags, some 120 in each 40 minute show.

When, in the same season (21 February 2001), Javier Cámara's plump and slow-witted Paco loses his job, the references become more barbed. He tells Carlota, apparently oblivious to his own plight, that Spain is the "land of opportunity" and that the Partido Popular has lowered the rate of unemployment. The cast cluck about the notorious intrusiveness of the Spanish paparazzi. But they are well versed in the gossip on local celebrities. And when pictures of Diana kissing her new girlfriend, a washed up actress, are about to appear in the press, the latter is delighted by this intrusion on their privacy which will bring valuable publicity. Diana dumps her, saying she wants a relationship with a partner not a limited company.

Some sensitive social issues are focused around a new character: the moustachioed El Frutero ("The Greengrocer"), so benighted he does not even have a name. El Frutero employs an illegal Peruvian worker in his shop. But it's not because he can pay him less than a Spaniard. It lends an "exotic touch." After all, he says, parodying the well intentioned political correctness of *Médico de familia*, "the future is cultural *mestizaje*." But even this outspoken racist reveals unexpected and self-deprecating ironies. When Gonzalo pretends to be gay in order to clinch a business deal with the representative of a chain of Irish bars (first shown 12 March 2003), El Frutero confesses that he's slept with girls who are uglier than the cute young businessman. And when the latter discovers the truth, he attacks Gonzalo's ethics by calling attention to his dress sense: even Paco Clavel (the famously camp entertainer) wouldn't be caught dead in the lacy black T-shirt which Gonzalo chose for his gay masquerade.

The moral here is especially ambivalent: Gonzalo protests, rightly if hypocritically, that sexual preference has nothing to do with business. But unable to profit from the new cosmopolitan trend for ersatz Irishness, he is forced to be content with the familiar "domestic brands" (*productos nacionales)* in his bar. Touching lightly on the themes of age, class, and nationality (the same ones that were dutifully explored just a few years earlier in *Médico de familia)*, *7 Vidas* sweetens its liberal politics with a distinctive aesthetics. Like the characters, the target audience is expected to be as comfortable and confident in a gay bar as they are in their choice of wardrobe.

Indeed, while nobody watched *Médico de familia* for the clothes, *7 Vidas*, often praised for its topicality (*actualidad)*, is conspicuously well dressed. The stylist takes care to follow seasonal changes in fashion: in 2001 the cast wore neutral solids; in 2003 their tops broke out in diagonal stripes and international slogans ("Girl 60," "Shaolin Football" [sic: for the Hong Kong martial arts comedy *Shaolin Soccer*]). The skirt lengths of the women (not to mention their knee high suede boots) are said to set trends. Twenty-something Vero gives a name check to Zara, the Spanish high street fashion brand with the fastest turnaround of catwalk trends in the world. While working-class Aída is dressed by Sepu (a Woolworth-like chain store) she is neither caricatured nor patronized as is her equivalent in *Médico de familia*, the Andalusian housekeeper Juani. In spite of their urban sophistication, the middle-class characters are not so blinded by fashion as to be indifferent to proletarian survivors, as wounded as they are by unsettled social conditions.

7 Vidas, which regularly features cameos from sport or media celebrities, is thus as media literate as it is socially compassionate, with several characters working in the cultural industries (TV, music, journalism). Three episodes explore this mix of social comment and ironic self-referentiality that is distinctively urban. One episode first shown on 7 March 2001 (and rerun in March 2003) begins with the women sceptically perusing a women's magazine in the bar ("Who needs six ways to extend your eyelashes?"). When Carlota lightheartedly fills in a questionnaire with answers suggesting she is unsatisfied in bed, Gonzalo spends the rest of the episode attempting athletic and unsuccessful innovations in the bedroom (male sexuality is always fragile in *7 Vidas*). Meanwhile two parallel plotlines explore mother–son relationships. Alex, a journalist, is concerned by his sexually active mother's younger lover (Alex has had, we are told, "more fathers than the Constitution"). Stolid Paco refuses to reveal his distress when his own mother Sole suggests she should move from Madrid to the Canaries ("I haven't seen the sea since Moses parted it").

As the plotlines intersect, the sexual vanity of men and their continuing domestic dependence on women are explored in physical comedy: Gonzalo, Alex, and Paco attempt to demonstrate their superior sexual technique while doing the ironing. And verbal gags tease out the political and geographical dimensions of personal aspirations and relations: Sole's "dream of a lifetime" was not to retire conventionally to the sun but rather to "sing the Internationale stark naked in the Valle de los Caídos;" and she gently reminds her immature son that "the metro doesn't reach Tenerife." Eschewing easy hugs, the Sole–Paco tension is characteristically resolved through the media, when the mother hears the son tell a radio phone-in show about the feelings he cannot bring himself to admit directly to her. Aided by the subtlety of the performances (was it an accident that Javier Cámara would soon be playing a rather similar mother obsessed son in *Hable con ella?*), the episode swiftly and subtly modulates mood and tone, acting styles and genre conventions.

Another episode, this time from the tenth season (first broadcast 19 March 2003), is more farcical. Vero engages a hunky male cleaner, who is more assiduous with one kind of *polvo* ("fucking") than he is with the other ("dust"). She is forced to admit by the end that this convenient arrangement amounts to male prostitution. Back at the bar, El Frutero sells tickets to a lottery in aid of "syllepsis" (which is later correctly identified by another character as a rhetorical figure, not a disease). Sole puts the scam down to the Socialist Party in their desperation to raise political funds. And in a sarcastic depiction of television production with echoes of *All About Eve*, a younger actress attempts to steal Diana's part in what is clearly an appalling series. This plot strand of on-set rivalry at once comments ironically on *7 Vidas'* own difficulty in retaining successful characters and confirms the series' own artistic distinction as compared to the grotesquely overacted and clichéd show within the show. This is perhaps the most extreme example of the way in which self-reflection is undercut by self-irony and laughter dedramatizes narcissism.

Elsewhere the scriptwriters skilfully exploit the familiar motif of sexual tension in a touching episode screened on 2 April 2003, which is parallel to the *Médico de familia* episode in which Nacho fails to confess his love for Alicia. In the comic plotline Sergio's sexual pride is hurt (as Gonzalo's was earlier) when he reads Vero's list of best lovers in which his own rating is "could do better" (*mejorable*). Carlota has now split from Gonzalo but is pregnant with his child. At this sensitive moment Gonzalo is asked by his new girlfriend to move with her to a home far from the city centre. Once more spatial practices menace sentimental attachments. Carlota, for her part, has invented an imaginary boyfriend ("he's unbelievable").

In what could be a clichéd situation (and indeed was in *Médico de familia*) the scriptwriters succeed in skilfully frustrating our expectations. When Gonzalo confesses to his girlfriend that he is the father of another woman's child she is not angry but delighted: they can raise it together in the new chalet, complete with garden. By the end of the episode Gonzalo refuses to sign the mortgage papers for the new house, but he and Carlota have failed to confess their renewed love for each other. As in Passerini's account of courtly love, unrequited passion does not degrade but rather dignifies its object. Even the comic subplot is resolved in a sentimental education: it was not Sergio's inexpert sexual technique that moved Vero but rather his romantic gestures (a tender look in the eyes, a male jacket donated to cold shoulders). The quest to reconcile female freedom and female independence thus remains ongoing. But it is not just the women who try in vain to balance rationality and affectivity, autonomy and responsibility. The men suffer too as they become new subjects, caught between sexual objectification (providers of pleasure and insemination) and emotional insecurity (recipients of ambivalent or indecipherable messages from their partners).

Towards an ethics of care?

Both *Médico de familia* and *7 Vidas* suggest a revaluation of the domestic and familiar in relation to the feminine. But clearly the familiarity which television both feeds and reflects is subject to constant change. Nacho's benign liberalism is hardly comparable to Diana's screwball libertarianism. And while *Médico de familia* did feature gay characters in minor roles it is impossible to imagine a lesbian permanently installed in the comfortable home of the Martíns: suburban domesticity is not such a broad tent. While the change in topics is transparent, the shift in sensibility is more difficult to pin down. From the good intentions of *Médico de familia* to the postmodern irony of *7 Vidas* is some distance for the audience to travel in so short a time. Tele 5's website gives some indication of the pleasures and anxieties experienced by viewers: they love the "naturalness" of lesbian Diana; claim "not to watch television" except for this show; and long nostalgically for the return of past characters (Tele 5). In spite of the ironic framing of the series (the self-conscious credit sequence and knowing media references) viewers still feel an intimacy with and an affective investment in this novel fictional world.

In its stress on solidarity between diverse groups *7 Vidas'* urban camaraderie is perhaps as utopian as *Médico de familia's* suburban domesticity. Emilio Aragón, a classically trained composer, was not merely involved in the production of the sitcom, he also wrote its throaty theme tune. And it seems unlikely that a Zara-clad twenty year old would really hang out with a sixty-something retiree, however endearingly rebellious the latter might be. But while *Médico de familia* is nostalgic for lost forms of family, *7 Vidas* looks forward to new structures of feeling that remain controversial (in the episode first shown on 14 July 2002 Diana married a woman soldier). The contrast between these two ideological positions reveals that the social meanings of television cannot be reduced to those of its proprietors (both shows depend ultimately on Berlusconi); nor are they determined by the then current political climate (both were made under the Partido Popular). TV culture is relatively autonomous from both its industrial context and the government legislation that still frames that context.

The television environment did, however, change radically in the years 1995–2003. While the sitcom *7 Vidas* cost the network half the price of an in-house series drama, as a quality scripted product it was under threat from the rise of the cheap reality shows that were also pioneered by Tele 5. When Emilio Aragón launched his own new series in January 2002 he acknowledged both the increasingly competitive environment (hoping for a share of 26%, where *Médico de familia* had regularly reached 40%) and changes in Spanish domestic arrangements. Ditching the glasses and growing his hair, Aragón played an unmarried and at times unsympathetic teacher estranged from his family. As the producer-actor said himself, the story was based on "horizontal" rather than "vertical" relations (on friends, rather than fathers and sons) (Noticiasdenavarra), "a family concept more in accordance with current society [*la actualidad*]" (Fraguas 2003). It seems that topicality was now a bigger draw or a better bet than nostalgia.

I have suggested that TV can be read, like oral history, as a corrective to more formal chronicles of, say, political process. Certainly, it embodies in an acute and sometimes uncomfortable way the cohabitation of the rational (economic calculation) and the emotional (identification and desire). It is clearly difficult to read Spanish cinema without a knowledge of the television culture which envelops it: graduates of *7 Vidas* starred in such high profile projects as Almodóvar's *Todo sobre mi madre* (*All About My Mother*: Toni Cantó) and *Hable con ella* (*Talk to Her*: Javier Cámara), Julio Medem's *Lucía y el sexo* (*Sex and Lucía*: Paz Vega), and Emilio Martínez Lázaro's musical comedy *El otro lado de la cama* (*The Other Side of the Bed*: Guillermo Toledo and Paz Vega), the biggest success of 2002. Their big-screen performances are inevitably coloured by their familiar character profiles on the small screen. More domestic and everyday than cinema, however, TV is a subtle and precise barometer of a cultural identity, a specific national culture, and the congruence (or lack of it) between the two. Studies of production history reveal how intimate and continuous is the feedback into programmes by their prospective audiences. A collective field in which ideas, feelings, and relations circulate with some autonomy, TV has more fathers (and mothers) than the Constitution. To reject it as capitalist exploitation is to reconfirm the devaluation of a private sphere that has been bravely rehabilitated by some feminists.

In their different ways, both *Médico de familia* and *7 Vidas* restore to women rights to citizenship (to social participation and commentary) and rights to passion (to excess and disorder) that had been denied them by earlier versions of domesticity. This restitution, one of Passerini's aims, is what I call a politics of affect. But beyond this, Passerini and Pulcini (2002) seek "a new ethics (of care) and a new subjectivity (dialogical, relational)" (102). At its best, television fiction can not just represent such an ethics and such a subjectivity on screen, but can stimulate them amongst viewers. As Passerini has shown, such self-imaging may be all the more potent when seasoned (as in *7 Vidas*) with self-irony. The family plot would then be not a conspiracy against the public but rather an invitation to make national narratives in collaboration with it.

Works cited

Bourdieu, Pierre. *Distinction: A Social Critique of the Judgement of Taste*. London and New York: Routledge, 1984.

Passerini, Luisa. *Fascism in Popular Memory: The Cultural Experience of the Turin Working Class*. Cambridge: Cambridge University Press, 1987.

—. *Storie di donne e femministe*. Turin: Rosenberg & Sellier, 1991.

—. *Autobiography of a Generation: Italy, 1968*. Hanover, CT: Wesleyan University Press, 1996.

—. *Europe in Love, Love in Europe: Imagination and Politics in Britain Between the Wars*. London and New York: I. B. Tauris, 1999.

— and Pulcini, Elena. 'European feminine identity and the idea of passion in politics.' In Gabriele Griffin and Rosi Braidotti (eds), *Thinking Differently*. London and New York: Zed, 2002, 97–109.

Sánchez-Mellado, Luz. 'Las siete vidas de *7 Vidas*.' *El País*, *Semanal*, 2 March 2003, 52–9.

Smith, Paul Julian. *Contemporary Spanish Culture: TV, Fashion, Art, and Film*. Cambridge and Oxford: Polity, 2003.

Electronic sources

Aragón, Emilio, and Sánchez Navas, Gemma. 'El secreto de mi éxito.' *El Mundo: La Revista* 9 November 1997. Accessed 27 August 2003. www.el-mundo.es/larevista/num108/textos/medi.html

Collins, Richard. 'National culture: A contradiction in terms?'. *Canadian Journal of Communications* 16.2, 1991. Accessed 27 August 2003. www.wlu.ca/~wwwpress/jrls/cjc/BackIssues/16.2/collins.html

Espindola de Castro, Cosette. 'El discurso amoroso en *Médico de familia*.' Accessed 27 August 2003. www.aijic.com/comunica/comunica2/castro.htm

Fraguas, Marietta. 'Emilio Aragón vuelve en enero a TV con *Javier*, la nueva serie de Tele 5.' *Terra*. Accessed 27 August 2003. www.terra.es/ocio/articulo/html/oci13974.htm

Guadilla, David. 'Amparo Baró: protagonista de *7 Vidas*.' 16 March 2003. Accessed 27 August 2003.

http://servicios.elcorreodigital.com/vizcaya/pg030316/
prensa/noticias/Portada_VIZ/200303/16/VIZ-ACT-332.html

López Monjas, Chusa. 'Carmen Machi/Actriz: "En *7 vidas* recoge-
mos lo que dice la gente de la calle, y eso gusta".' 21 May 2003.
Accessed 27 August 2003. www.laverdad.es/panorama/
corazonprotagonista210503.htm

Muchatv. '*Médico de familia.*' Accessed 27 August 2003.
www.muchatv.com/serie.php?idserie=18

Noticiasdenavarra. 'Tele 5 estrena la serie *Javier ya no vive solo,*
sobre la vida de un profesor.' 13 January 2002.
Accessed 27 August 2003. www.noticiasdenavarra.com/
ediciones/20020113/television/index.php

Paramountcomedy. '*Médico de familia*: la serie.'
www.paramountcomedy.es/series/mdf/mdf_1.htm

Passerini, Luisa. 'Becoming a subject in the time of the death of
the subject.' Fourth European Feminist Research Conference,
September 2000. Accessed 27 August 2003.
www.women.it/4thfemconf/lunapark/passerini.htm

Popular Memory Group. 'Popular Memory: Theory, Politics,
Method.' Accessed 27 August 2003.
http://xroads.virginia.edu/ ~DRBR/memory.html

Rodríguez, Mercedes. 'Gonzalo de Castro: "*7 vidas* es una de las
pocas series que hacen reír".' 13 July 2003. Accessed 27 August
2003. http://servicios.laverdad.es/albacete/pg030713/prensa/
noticias/Television/200307/13/MUR-TV-108.html

Tele 5. '*Vidas* vuelve con nuevos personajes: opiniones de los
usuarios.' Accessed 27 August 2003. www.Tele 5.es/rdesar-
rollo_ 10482.htm

Todotv. 'Estrella... El adiós de *Médico de familia.*' Accessed 27
August 2003. http://todotv.metropoliglobal.com/cr-ee17.html

Urjc. 'Emilio Aragón Alvarez.' Universidad Rey Juan Carlos.
Accessed 27 August 2003.
www.urjc.es/z_files/af_alumn/af10/ ficheros/profesorado/
emilioaragon.htm

3

The movida relocated: press, chronicle, novel

Temporal geographies

There would seem to be a consensus about the transition to democracy, at least amongst Spanish cultural scholars based in the US. It goes like this: the horrors of the past were silenced after the death of Franco; this repression caused a trauma which later returned as cold turkey (*mono*), melancholia, or wound; and this return of the repressed signals an inability to exorcise the past which compromises Spanish democracy up to the present day.

Although such studies tend to focus on literature and cinema, they lay claim to an interpretation of Spanish history and society, beyond cultural analysis. Thus one is published in a series called 'Sociología y política' (Vilarós 1998); and others boast on their covers images based on El Valle de los Caídos (Medina Domínguez 2001) or even Adolfo Suárez (Moreiras-Menor 2002), leader of the doomed UCD, the first party to govern after the death of Franco. However, they do not draw on sociological research for the period (on trends in work, family structure, or attitudes to democracy); nor do they attempt to reconstruct an extensive "cultural field" of the type produced for France by Bourdieu. Rather the theoretical touchstones are Debord and Baudrillard on the society of the spectacle and the simulacrum and (a key text) Freud on mourning and melancholia.

Angel Loureiro (2003) has recently suggested that this type of model privileges politics to the exclusion of other factors. Certainly, it tends to reduce politics to the parliamentary system, and thus neglects the forms of political agency that are implicit in everyday life. However there is also a question of the criteria of inclusion for those literary and cinematic texts which are held to exemplify and reconfirm the political thesis of the return of the repressed. A certain canon has emerged. Figures as distinct as Juan Goytisolo and Leopoldo María Panero (poet son of the official bard of Francoism) are positive models, in that they overtly display trauma (melancholy and wounds) in their engagement with the past. Conversely, but consistently, figures such as Almodóvar and poet Ana María Rossetti, are negative models: their apparent passion for the present (for the superficial, sensual, and consumerist) is held to be a disavowal of past trauma and, thus, unwitting testimony to the same horrors that are directly addressed by others. Mourning and melancholia thus join hands with spectacle and simulacrum in a metaphorical model which is as capacious as it is versatile.

What of this psychoanalytic model? Critics of the transition coincide in claiming that Spaniards are in thrall, albeit unwittingly, to a lost object: Francisco Franco. Freud's founding theory, however, does not seem to correspond to historical circumstances in Spain. For example, Freud writes in the opening of his essay that mourning is the "reaction to the loss of a loved person, or to the loss of some abstraction which has taken the place of one, such as one's country, liberty, an ideal, and so on" (Freud 1991, 252). Melancholia is, of course, a "pathological" version of this loss. Yet few scholars suggest that Franco was widely loved by the Spanish populace, as befits the internalized object of melancholia; nor do they go as far as to suggest that liberty was lost on his death (although they continually impugn Spanish democracy). Even if dictatorship had become an "addiction" from which the Spanish had to be weaned or an open "wound" which would require time to heal, Freud's description of the melancholic does not coincide with the common view of cultural producers in the period. The intense sociability of, say, the movida madrileña is incompatible with the mourner's "cessation of interest in the outside world ... [and] inhibition of activity" (*ibid.*, 252). The relentless self-promotion of such figures as Almodóvar, universally thought to be exemplary, is difficult to reconcile with the "self-reproach," "disturbance of self-regard," and "inhibition of the ego" (*ibid.*, 252) typical of the melancholic. Likewise an "excessive devotion to mourning which leaves nothing over for other purposes" is belied by the explosion of cultural activity in all media which greeted the death of the dictator.

Given that Franco's demise was hardly unexpected, and indeed had been anticipated for many years before, it seems possible that Spaniards were well on the way to completing Freud's demand of "reality-testing," namely that "libido be withdrawn from its attachment to that object" (Freud 1991, 253). After all, this attachment was, at the very least, ambivalent. The "free and uninhibited" ego of Freud's successful mourner seems closer to the movida than ego-loss of the melancholic, whose libido has fatally regressed (*ibid.*, 267). Although exploration of the traumas of history was not infrequent in Spanish culture of the transition (indeed, the period picture would soon prove a characteristic genre of Socialist cinema), it might be argued that it is not the artists of the 1970s and 1980s but the cultural critics of the 1990s and 2000s who are guilty, like Freud's melancholic, of "psychically prolong[ing]" the lost object (*ibid.*, 253).

I would suggest, then, that we adopt a more sympathetic attitude to the cultural production of the transition and, indeed, to its political process. Attention would then shift from mourning and melancholia to the less fashionable themes of life, liberty, and the pursuit of pleasure, if not happiness. One way to do so is to change and extend the corpus or object of study by first examining primary sources of the period, such as the press, and contrasting them with the chronicles and novels which look back on the same material. Another way is to shift methodology away from parliamentary process (the deficiencies, real or imagined, of Suárez and Felipe González) to the more fragile and flexible practices of everyday life. Arguably, the latter are more central to the success of democratic citizenship than formal institutions. To this end I propose a theoretical move from psychoanalysis to cultural geography and, more precisely, to urbanism and the much discussed notion of time-space.

Mutatis mutandis, the return of the Labour Party to power in the UK in 1997 presents some structural parallels with the triumph of the Socialists in Spain in 1982. Just as the city would prove central to the transition, so an urban renaissance was held to be key to social and cultural change in Britain. Geographers in the UK were spurred to contribute to this debate on at least three levels: practical proposals for policy change; more general accounts of "spatial formations" in cities; and theoretical versions of "temporalized space" or rhythm as played out in the urban site. Although they are clearly interconnected, for the purposes of exposition I will take these three areas in turn.

Reacting to the report by the prestigious architect (Lord) Richard Rogers (*Towards an Urban Renaissance*, 1999), three British geographers offer some pointers towards *Cities for the Many, Not for the Few*

(Amin, Massey, and Thrift 2000). Noting the new Labour government has no "overall conception of 'urban citizenship,'" they stress
that in a still centralized state, where devolution was only now being
contemplated, cities were both "seedbeds of the local" and, in their
hybridity, inherently "conflictual" (ibid., vi). While they welcome the
"enthusiasm" of the Rogers report for the potential of cities (rare in
a country with a long history of anti-urbanism) and the shift from
the sprawling congestion of the US to "thriving European cities" as
a model for sustainability and human scale (ibid., 1), they suggest
two inadequacies. The first is that the report is "overly design-led"
and subscribes to "environmental determinism" (ibid., 3). Just as
local governments in the 1960s trusted to concrete tower blocks to
solve social problems and private corporations of the 1980s put
their faith in glass towers, so this new urban renaissance relies too
heavily on the quality of building design. The second inadequacy is
the "presupposition of attainable urban harmony:"

The new compact city will strike a balance between nature, built environment, and society, between private, public, and community, between
work, travel, home, shopping, and play. This harmony is based on a rose-
tinted evocation of the centres of selected European cities – their historical architecture, busy markets, small shops, cafes and squares, mixed
buildings and residential blocks and proud citizens. (ibid., 4)

Unfortunately, this utopia is characteristic neither of British
metropolises nor of the outer areas of European cities. Moreover, the
urban "vibrancy" held to be typical of mainland Europe is founded
on "diversity in close proximity," which is itself ambivalent in its
effects. While it can lead to "creative intermingling, cultural mix-
ture, and exploratory potential," it also results in "a desperate
search for privacy, sanctuary, and anonymity" (ibid., 4).

How, then, are we to imagine cities in ways helpful for public
policy? The first general principle is that cities are not things but
processes or interactions whose ends cannot be predicted. The
second is that the interaction in cities is peculiarly intense, once
more with unpredictable results (Amin, Massey, and Thrift 2000, 8).
For example, a specialized area (e.g. a "gay village") may prove to be
exclusive in both positive and negative senses, manifesting either
"exclusivity" or "exclusion" (ibid., 9). A third principle is that "cities

are essentially dynamic" (*ibid.*, 10). However, as open and interconnected spatial phenomena, they are also highly "varied," and must be studied for their "individualities" (*ibid.*, 11–14). One vital aspect here is "recognition for the increasing centrality of the social/civic economy centred around not for profit activities ... [as an] alternative to the formal economy" (*ibid.*, 28).

This urban imagining gives rise to "rights to the city." Social expression and participation often offer "non-instrumental gains" (Amin, Massey, and Thrift 2000, 32), such as public access to open spaces. The authors propose "hedonism without consumerism" (*ibid.*, 36) as the "driving force of a new politics of transformation" (*ibid.*, 37). Their "interest in pleasure [is] not gratuitous [and] not a prioritization of individual rights over social obligations [but rather a way to] inculcate civic values." Through pleasure, individuals can be offered "the possibility of becoming something/someone else" beyond "the traditional politics of prescription and elite designation" (*ibid.*, 38). Cities, they say, are already "replete" with this unfocused energy, full as they are of "creativity and innovation." To sum up:

> We need to recognize the role of cities as places of socialization and sociability beyond riverside cafes, shopping mall atria, and bijou restaurants ... [to] acknowledge and encourage the vast network of everyday associations of sociability which already exists ... beyond the life of firms and work, melancholy and alienation, state and other institutions of governance ... We need to recognize spaces of democracy that lie beyond democratic state and representative politics ... Cities are massive reservoirs of institutionalized activity, around which urban democracy can be built and extended. (*ibid.*, 42)

Beyond these particular policy proposals, many of which are as relevant for high density Spain as they are for suburban Britain, general accounts of spatial formations are also important. Qualifying the "spatial turn," or even "spatial imperialism" of recent theory (May and Thrift 2001, 1, 2), some of the same scholars call for "geographies of temporality." Four kinds of time intersect dynamically with urban space: the rhythms of the natural world; those of social discipline (both religious and secular); instruments and devices (such as the VCR); and texts, which serve as "vehicles of translation" for time (*ibid.*, 3–4). The authors argue that "social time is made and remade according to social practices operating within and across each of these domains" (*ibid.*, 5). Time-space is thus by no means dualistic or dichotomous. Rather it serves as "the essential unit of geography." Adapting Marx, Nigel Thrift writes: "The frozen circumstances of space only come alive when the melody of time is played" (1996, 1).

In "Rhythms of the city: Temporalized space and motion", Mike Crang (2001) goes further. For Crang the "intersection of lived time, time as represented, and urban space" is typical of everyday practice (187). Multiple temporalities collide: dominant forms of linearity or even simultaneity overlay "quieter cycles on daily, weekly, annual rhythms that continue to structure the everyday" (*ibid.*, 189). The urban place or site is actually composed through "patterns of these multiple beats" (*ibid.*, 190). Its plural rhythms include not only the trend towards acceleration so often cited by theorists, but other phenomena, such as the "colonization of the night – the steady movement of social life into the dark" (*ibid.*, 191). Again the much discussed "non-stop city" may break down "family time" ("the demise of 'meal times'"). But it also allows "new rhythmic groupings [to] emerge ... transient, episodic affinities and comings together [in] neo-tribes." The latter rework old collective temporalities without "locking into the solidarities of tradition." The rhythms of the city lead inevitably to both the formation of collective groups and their "dissolution, fragmentation, and reformation." Urban living is thus both a "rhythmic composition" and a "realm of shattered, fragmented times" (*ibid.*, 191). Finally, the "polychronic city" is not just a question of "routes, routines, and paths" (*ibid.*, 192) but also one of "velocities, directions, turnings, detours, exits, and entries" (*ibid.*, 206). If urban space is to dance, then, then it must be "temporalized" (*ibid.*, 200).

La Luna de Madrid (*The Moon of Madrid*): the pleasures of urban apprenticeship

La Luna begins with a smile. The first issue of the quintessential magazine of the movida (November 1983) features a typically stylish trompe l'oeuil photograph by Ouka Lele: a hand tears back a strip of wrapping paper behind which we see a woman's lipsticked mouth and exposed teeth. With its large format (36 x 27cm) and extended length (72 pages), *La Luna* is a substantial document of the period, and remains so for the twenty issues which will be edited by Borja Casani. Aesthetically it is difficult to place. The art design is distinctive: the famous logo is based on 1960s-style space age lettering and the layout features semi-Vorticist diagonal placing of text and image. With its poor paper quality and limited colour (restricted to accents in tangerine, lime, and pink in the first three issues), *La Luna* positions itself between the well established glossies and the grubby Xeroxes of the new fanzines (*Penetración*, a carbon copy of UK punk originals, also began publication in 1983). Compared to its most obvious foreign precedents and equivalents, *La Luna* is less enamoured of celebrity than New York's *Interview*, which carried full colour star portraits by Warhol on its cover, and less devoted to cutting-edge design than London's *The Face*.

The smile is significant. *La Luna* shows little sign of mourning, melancholia, or *desencanto*. Indeed it is at once fascinated by the outside world and free and uninhibited in its egotism. The personification of this optimism is its most famous and enduring feature: Patti Diphusa, the chronicles of a gloriously hedonistic porno star, authored by Almodóvar and impersonated by Fabio McNamara in a series of outrageous photo portraits by Pablo Pérez Mínguez. Patti is a creature of the present. She exclaims to the editor that she loves *La Luna* already, even though he confesses that the first issue has yet to appear. As she explains, when she likes something, she likes it right away. *La Luna*'s secret, then, is this absolute contemporaneity: from the very beginning it sought to bring together in a magic circle of distinction the best and brightest in the multiple media of music, fashion, visual arts, and literature.

The contents of the first issue are, however, heterogeneous. Through a curious accident of the layout, Patti Diphusa is placed opposite the lead interview. This is with poet Leopoldo Panero, famously damaged victim of a Francoist father, who speaks directly from the mental institution (his ravaged face looms out from the grainy full page photo). The magazine also initiates a series called "Náufragos." Here politicians of both left and right, "shipwrecked" by the vicissitudes of the transition, are also featured. They begin with Enrique Líster, the "old Red general." Even a lengthy interview with Guillermo Pérez Villalta, the emblematic painter of the period, is structured around an interrogation of the past. One of his recent paintings is explicated with reference to its creative history (working practices and sketches), its personal background (a love affair and illness), and its art-historical influences (from Velásquez to Sorolla). In the second issue the painters Costus, retrospectively haloed by early deaths from AIDS and suicide, will recount a professional history which, like that of Pérez Villalta, testifies more to hard work and sociability than to psychic wounds or trauma.

The self-conscious creation of a community is clear even in the pastime section: new readers are invited to identify the faces of thirty figures of the movida. A "self-portrait" feature also allows luminaries to present their own public image to the emerging audience (the first is photographer Pérez Mínguez). But this process is inseparable from the city. Future competitions will feature unidentified gates and clocks ("The Time of Madrid"), testing and schooling readers in the built environment of Madrid (no. 3, January 1984; no. 7, May 1984). Even when Pérez Mínguez shows himself bathing in the Mediterranean, he wears, playfully and ironically, a Madrid T-shirt, complete with iconic bear and tree.

Perhaps the most unusual and explicit example of urban apprenticeship is the appearance in each issue of minutely detailed drawings of individual buildings, which readers are encouraged to cut out and keep. Beginning with central sites such as the Plaza del Callao the section will soon light out for less familiar locations (the muddled intersection of Cuatro Caminos, the distant and undistinguished office buildings of the Plaza de Castilla). This is not just an example of the inculcation of civic pride (of renewed pleasure in the detail of familiar locations). It is also an investigation of urban function and history: the pseudonymous commentator ("Mieldeluna" or "Honeymoon") lists both the multiple uses of often insignificant buildings (housing, rented offices, small shops and cafes) and the aesthetic influences of their precisely dated construction (Parisian Beaux Arts, Chicago School modern, Castilian vernacular). Even the massive and ungainly Torre de Madrid, the product of untamed Francoist speculation, can be made "loveable" (*entrañable*), when subjected to this affectionate make over (no. 12, November 1984).

A seed-bed of the local (like the city itself), *La Luna* also serves to temporalize space. An extreme instance here is the agenda which takes up two pages of each issue and is first printed on a shadowy background of that most recognizable of monuments, the Puerta de Alcalá. The days remain empty, ready to be filled. Just as readers are invited to appropriate even the grandest of city spaces, rendered small and accessible when cut out and kept, so they are helped to structure their time: "léete la revista y búscate la vida" ("read the magazine and get yourself a life"). *La Luna* understands that space will dance only to the music of time. Hence its double role as geographical guide and chronicle of urban life. It is thus a key text for the translation of social time into social practice.

Two contributions to the first issue are vital here. The first is editor Borja Casani and literary editor José Tono Martinez's manifesto "Madrid 1984: ¿la posmodernidad?" (6–7). The magazine's starting point is precisely that of the intersection of time and space. The article opens, lyrically, as follows:

Parece como si algo hubiera muerto en este Madrid de otoño-invierno que se apresta de nuevo a introducirse, empujado por el frío, en sus viejas catacumbas visionarias infernales. (*ibid.*, 6)

It seems like something has died in this autumnal or wintry Madrid which, under the influence of the cold weather, is getting ready once more to slip into its old visionary and hellish catacombs.

Autumnal melancholy (a reminder of the continuing presence of the slow natural cycle in the frantic rhythm of the city) gives way at once, however, to optimism. After all, the article may begin with an unspecified death, but it is named for a year that has yet to begin. The authors state that "something" (again unspecified) has changed. For the first time in its recent history Madrid can take the initiative in life, art, and creativity and can make its first serious incursion into the "so-called avant-gardes." But what is significant is that this radical change is not imposed from above by a small group of intellectuals as in the past, but comes up from the street, where it can be seen in people and even "clothing." The whole city has become avant-garde and taken on a new attitude: carefree, jovial, curious, and sceptical. The new attitude has two characteristics. First of all, it is urban and thus difficult to export, unless it is to other cities. Secondly, it understands art to be not an object but a style. Paris, London, and New York have had their times: now is Madrid's moment to export culture when for so long it has merely imported from abroad.

This rose-tinted self-regard, the sign of a free and uninhibited ego, is qualified by a sceptical irony. Madrid's advantage is its "ruins:" in a fragile economy artists will flourish, since architects, for example, lacking work, will turn into painters (first issue, 7). And the Spanish capital, suddenly cut down to size, is surely the "tallest dwarf city in the world." There remains however in the manifesto a justified pride in the success of the city's struggle against social and aesthetic taboos and a certainty that "something has been over-come" (*algo ha sido superado*). The art of such a time should appeal to the criterion of quality, rather than novelty; and its attitude should be that of "laughter" in a doubtful present. The utopia pro-posed here, then, is one of democratic citizenship, which looks to the future and is vitally engaged by the present, but does not deny the past. Something, the editors of *La Luna* tell us, has died; but some-thing has been overcome. Significantly, this possibility of overcom-ing is precisely what is denied by the international theory of postmodernism (Vattimo 1988, passim). Spanish versions of such concepts must thus be carefully and sensitively localized, read for their individualities, if they are to give up their true meanings.

Magazines are both word and image; and the second exemplary text of the first issue is the opening instalment of a wordless graphic novel called *Manuel* by the little known artist called simply "Rodrigo." *Manuel*, which ran over six full pages until issue 16, is an enigmatic and suggestive story of love between bearded men (the physical type is very precise). The unnamed protagonist falls for the taller, darker, and even hairier Manuel, an apparently heterosexual man. Countering the acceleration of city life, Rodrigo boldly post-pones a narrative whose readers are already constrained by the reg-ular, but infrequent, monthly rhythm: it is not until issue 15 that the two men make love and even then it is only perhaps in fantasy.

Unlike his better-known counterparts, the lyrical Ceesepe and the mock-naïve Mariscal, also founding contributors to *La Luna*, Rodrigo is a technically perfect draftsman, having trained as an architect. And he is highly innovative, constantly playing with the grid format of the comic. Most significant, however, is his focus on the spatial formations of everyday life in the city. Opening with a wholly black image, the first page continues with an extreme close up of a hand lighting a match and a candle. We then pull back to see a contented protagonist (the spitting image of the artist himself) lying back on his pillow flanked, like a secular saint, by serried ranks of candles (Figure 6). The format changes to elongated rectangles, mimicking the shape of a mirror, as he playfully tries on costumes, discarding check shirts and polka dot ties for less showy plain shirt and trousers (Figure 7). Making his way to the Noviciado Metro entrance (a meticulously detailed portrait of the street facades), he goes down to the train (shown in a lateral cutaway) (Figure 8). His destination is the swimming pool. In the final full-page image, his face, emerging from the water, is seen from between the muscular legs of the otherwise invisible Manuel, who is standing by the pool. Looking longingly up out of frame, the protagonist is a new Sebastian, torso pierced by arrows from the perfect Art Nouveau cherubs entwined around the new beloved's name.

Rodrigo testifies, obliquely (even mutely), to the democratic citizenship that *La Luna's* editors so proudly announced. He and his character exercise without fear their right to the city (their right to social expression and participation), taking advantage of access to public spaces (streets, stations, and swimming pools) to stage a touching gay romance. The geography of the city extends, however, beyond the public sphere (diverse in its close proximity) into private space: the character's basement apartment is almost literally his sanctuary, illuminated as it is by church candles. *Manuel* celebrates the pleasures of city solitude as it does those, better known perhaps, of the chance urban encounter. And its hedonism is untainted by consumerism. In interview with *La Luna* (no. 7, May 1984) Rodrigo confessed what was transparently obvious from his work: that he took intense delight in walking the city streets and in the details of the built environment, most especially the incongruously rich ornaments of the "theatrical" buildings of the Gran Vía. But this is no environmental determinism. For Rodrigo's urban spaces are not frozen fetishes, but are rather made to dance to temporal rhythms, both natural and social. As the couple talk by the pool in the second instalment the evening shadow falls over them in successive images; colonizing the night, the two men move social life into the dark when they go from pool to discotheque. In the episodes that follow, where chronology and geography are often wilfully fluid and confused, Rodrigo overlays the multiple fragmented beats of urban time onto the relatively regular rhythmic composition of the monthly magazine.

I say "relatively regular" because part of La Luna's particular charm is that it cheerfully disregards calendar time when it wishes. Issue number 2 (December 1983) promises that "the whole year will be a carnival;" and number 4 (February 1984) claims that "the cold is just a shaggy dog story [*cuento chino*]" and sends a model out on the frigid city streets in a monokini. Two numbers bear the date "April 1985" on the cover (nos. 16, 17) and the spoof issue 44 (published in June 1984, not 1987 as it boasts on the cover) stands in for number 8 (interestingly, the future includes a new Civil War at the gates of Madrid and a tottering skyscraper made up of fragments of existing buildings). Summer issues show a sweaty Madrid salaryman soaking his feet in the Plaza Mayor or a trendy sun lover who sets up his deck chair and parasol on city rail tracks (nos. 9–10, July–August 1984). Once more time, space, and urban pleasure are inextricable.

But if there seems little mourning or melancholia in La Luna (even Rodrigo takes great pleasure in his frustrated love affair), then nor can the magazine be dismissed as pure spectacle or simulacrum. As I argued earlier, special issues on such topics as "postmodernity," "the flight of reality" (no. 3, January 1984), or indeed "simulation" (no. 13, December 1984), need to be reread within a Spanish context. Indeed, they are interspersed with apparently contrary themes such as "Radical space" (no. 12, November 1984) and "Being modern" (no. 14, January 1985). A lengthy interview with Eduardo Haro Ibars (no. 5, March 1984) has the famously doomed gay activist and author (who would indeed die later of AIDS) stress that, contrary to his public image, he is "sensible" and politically committed. Indeed his role model is Juan Goytisolo (who would also be interviewed by La Luna [no. 20, July–August 1985]). "Postmodernism" in 1980s Madrid is thus a broad church indeed.

Even if we can no longer experience the excitement of the first subscribers, the accumulated effect of the magazine remains temporal. Month by month, issue by issue, La Luna drew on a reservoir of urban creativity and innovation that at once acknowledged and encouraged a network of everyday associations of sociability. If that time-space complex sometimes seemed exclusive, then it offered readers the fantasy at least of joining the magic circle: if you could recognize the gates and clocks of Madrid, then surely one day your picture would appear amongst those of the *modernos* shown socializing at the famous picnics and parties meticulously organized and faithfully documented by the magazine. While such neo-tribes would prove transient, their routes and paths were infinite. Certainly, *La Luna* provided ample evidence of the possibility of becoming something or someone else in the city.

Sólo se vive una vez (You Only Live Once): rhythms of the city

I have suggested, then, that *La Luna* served, like the city itself, as a temporalized space and perhaps an education in democratic citizenship. Its blurry and now faded pages testify to extreme diversity in close proximity. *La Luna*'s uniqueness in both form and content (subsequent magazines could not equal its influence) is matched by an unprecedented chronicle of the period published a decade later: José Luis Gallero's *Sólo se vive una vez: esplandor y ruina de la movida madrileña (You Only Live Once: Splendour and Ruins of the Movida Madrileña)* (1991). This is a rare example of oral history in Spain, its nearest parallels being Jean Stein and George Plimptons's *Edie: An American Biography* (1984), an encyclopaedic and polyglossic account of the Warhol era, and Jon Savage's *England's Dreaming* (2002), a more traditional history of punk. *Sólo*'s editor, who admits he did not participate in the movida, adopts a wilfully eccentric format. His book is composed of conversations which took place in 1990 and 1991, loosely divided into sections (the first and longest is dominated by *La Luna*'s editor Borja Casani). Transcriptions of these interviews are interrupted apparently at random by sidebars and boxes quoting press sources from the period. There are also interpolated tables of data, whose periodization is, as ever, inconsistent. The chronology (a minute list of concerts, gallery openings, and parties) runs from 1977 to 1984; the list of media (from TV shows to fanzines) from 1979 to 1984; and the discography is restricted to the "historical period," here given as 1980–83. The multivocal format, in which distinct voices complement and contradict one another, is thus matched by a disputed temporal framework.

Sólo's voices and faces (there is an excellent selection of photographs) include all those we have seen and heard in *La Luna*: Borja

Casani and Ouka Lele, Fabio and Panero, Pérez Villalta and Pérez Mínguez. Those no longer alive but frequently invoked (the collection is dedicated to the memory of those who "fell" in the 1980s) include the painters Costus and the writer Haro Ibars. As in *La Luna*, and appropriately for a movement which claimed to value style over substance, *Sólo*'s format is significant. The text begins in mid-conversation on a foldout inside the front cover and a footnote alerts us to the fact that a previous discussion had gone unrecorded, thus requiring a repeated return to the point of departure. The editor's introduction is postponed until page 9. The cover image is a handsome print by Dis Berlín: a stylized street ascends to a nightclub, door invitingly open, as a single pedestrian swings around a last lamppost. In the background looms a 1950s-style geometric skyline, cut out against an electric sky with a crescent moon. Starting in medias res, the text of *Sólo* suggests that the movida, like the city, was not a thing, but a process, which has always already begun; and showing a nocturnal street scene on its cover, the chronicle signals that this ongoing history will be one of time-space, a geography of temporality. And while the dedication and subtitle hint at mortality (although "ruins" were, as we have seen, vindicated for their positive potential as early as 1983), the title itself stresses rather the unique and unrepeatable value of a human life.

The first voice, that of Borja Casani, is juxtaposed with the words of his manifesto, written in the previous decade. Borja Casani continues to defend the newness of the movida and its overcoming of the old. The first issues of *La Luna*, he claims, were "prophetic," in that they anticipated the arrival and "explosion" of "Spanishness" (*lo español*) in Spain. While there was no group consciousness amongst participants, there was a "consciousness of Madrid:" reviled, centralist, ordinary (*corriente*) as it was (first issue, 1). Now he claims that the promotion of Madrid as rival to New York and London, a boosterism much attacked by sceptics at the time, was just commercial or cynical in intent: a successful means to achieve notoriety. Yet still Borja Casani praises the genuine achievements of the movida, such as the bringing together of diverse social classes (*ibid.*, 2) in spite of the exclusivity of the little band at its centre. The movida's conditions of possibility were both spatial and temporal: the unusual presence in a compact Madrid of masses of people in the street and their equally stubborn refusal to submit to the social discipline of "European" timetables. Rather they combined work and fun, showing up at the office at 8.30am after staying out all night (*ibid.*, 7).

For Borja Casani the precision of this time-space practice is matched by the peculiarity of the cultural and political field at *La Luna*'s launch in 1983. After the triumph of the Socialists, he says, there was a "turn to culture" and away from politics, which had now, with the dominance of a single party, become "boring" (first issue, 8). While the established press needed pictures and copy to fill its new cultural supplements, the newly installed Socialists needed artistic innovation to testify to their modernity (*ibid.*, 8, 14). But this does not mean that the magazine was pure simulacrum, the product of a deracinated society of the spectacle. Rather it remained fiercely urban, even local: it had arisen at a *tertulia*, that most traditional Spanish form of sociality, and was staffed by friends from Borja Casani's barrio (*ibid.*, 11). And Casani qualifies his earlier quip about Madrid as a "dwarf." Here he calls attention to the restricted geographical area and high population density in the capital, praising the everyday practice, so taken for granted and so impossible elsewhere, of the chance encounter on the city street which leads to a beer in a bar (*ibid.*, 16).

Casani continues to vindicate the neighbourhood bars and the parties hosted by the magazine (which he claims lost huge amounts of money) as not merely hedonistic, but rather creative sources and spaces of sociability: "todo el mundo relacionado por la copa" (first issue, 19). Moreover, while the movida was attacked by the Left for being made up of conservatives, bourgeois, and queers, he champions homosexuals of the period as being an index of newly acquired freedom (the "absolute avant-garde" [*ibid.*, 20]) and defends political "ambiguity" against the "intolerance" of both sides (*ibid.*, 25). I would argue, then, that the movida can be accused of apoliticism only if the political is restricted to formal governance and to a Socialism that was to be as "shipwrecked" by power as the old generals were by the transition. Its bars and parties are neither the displacement of historical mourning nor the efflorescence of pure spectacle but rather spatial formations of intensely creative intermingling.

This pluralism, which Borja Casani defends not as postmodern fragmentation but rather as individualism ("unique, unrepeatable"), is reconfirmed by *Sólo*'s multiple chronicle as a whole. Even after a decade of loss, the introduction can claim that "everything" has remained from the period (first issue, 9). The many voices of the conversations, circling in different directions, taking different detours, yet always returning to the same places, point to a spatial turn or even to a spatial imperialism. All agree that central to the movement as a whole was the Costus house in Calle de la Palma in the old heart of the city. Here the "nucleus" of the group hung out, while newcomers and veterans staged repeated entrances and exits. This jealously guarded private space, variably permeable to chosen actors, served as a sanctuary (it was even known as the "convent"), a domestic location modelled ironically on that of the seamstresses (*costureras*) whose labour served as an inspiration for the industrious painters. But the "convent," often compared to Warhol's Factory, was loosely linked with less exclusive public spaces: the famed bars and nightclubs of the Rock-Ola, Marquee, and Astoria.

These locations proved relatively durable (although Costus moved temporarily to Mexico and Rock-Ola was closed as early as March 1985 [Castilla 1994]). But their regular rhythm is crosscut or overlain by unique, punctual events: *La Luna*'s striptease party (the only one to turn a profit); and, contradicting Madrid's proud independence of the old cultural capitals London and New York, Siouxsie and the Banshees' concert and the party given for Warhol by wealthy art lovers the March brothers. Although contradictory accounts are given of these events, the consensus is that the spectacular parties hosted by the Marches and others testified to the exploratory potential of the movida, the way in which punk kids could mingle with wealthy aesthetes and each draw some benefit from the other. Sociability thus led to socialization in briefly democratic spaces (nightclubs and villas) that facilitated transient affinities beyond state intervention and corporate exploitation.

There is also consensus on the fact that during the movida no-one made any money. Indeed this seems to be a necessary, if not sufficient, condition for admission to the inner circle. By the time Almodóvar achieved financial success, the golden age is said to be over. Rather than reading this as a failure, however, I would propose that the multiple practices of the movida constitute an early example of the social economy. While political economists have claimed that even now the social economy is relatively rare in Spain (Amin,

Cameron, and Hudson 2002, 11), their definition of the concept is strangely familiar:

[N]on-profit activities designed to combat social exclusion through socially useful goods sold in the market and which are not provided by the state or the private sector. The social economy generates jobs and entrepreneurship by meeting social needs and very often by deploying the socially excluded. (*ibid.*, vii)

Clearly, participants in the movida did not intend to be poor nor hope to be socially useful. Costus in particular suffered greatly from their poverty and Borja Casani frequently admits to a desire for wealth which the labour he put into his magazine did not afford him. The position of the movida *modernos* was, however, structurally similar to that of the social (or civic) workers. Poised between the different but equally compromising constraints of the public and private sectors, both attempt to market goods that deploy and employ socially excluded sectors of the urban population. A typically marginal figure like Rodrigo, who had received many rejections before his graphic novel was published so prominently by *La Luna* and whose work featured in a group exhibition sponsored by the magazine, simply drops off the map in the following decade. In spite of such losses and defeats, ably chronicled by the survivors in *Sólo*, we can reread the polychronic, non-stop city it describes as a rich producer of social goods and civic values.

Madrid ha muerto (*Madrid Has Died*): transient tribes

Luis Antonio de Villena's novel on the movida, *Madrid ha muerto: esplendor y caos de una ciudad feliz de los ochenta* (*Madrid Has Died: Splendour and Chaos of a Happy City of the 1980s*), was first published in 1999. Drenched in mourning, melancholia, and masochistic nostalgia, it evokes the pleasures of the 1980s from the perspective of the supposed horrors of the following decade, when sadness and emptiness had replaced the joy and plenitude of a golden age. The fatality of the title (a phrase attributed to designer Manuel Piña, a future casualty of AIDS) is thus juxtaposed with the happy urbanism of the subtitle (where, rewriting Balzac's histories of Parisian life, "splendour" is linked not to "misery" but rather to creative "chaos"). Something of this sense of both romance and dissolution is shown in the period image which graces the cover: Ceesepe's typically romantic "Golfo durmiendo" ("Hoodlum Sleeping") (1984). Here the handsome young man of the title rests his head on the tiles of a roof as his lower body appears to levitate above the candy coloured city. Behind him we recognize, fancifully transformed, the already theatrical buildings of the Gran Vía, here celebrated and deconstructed as tottering towers, layers of classical columns and pediments topped by cupolas. As in Dis Berlín's night scene on the cover of *Sólo*, also, a crescent moon hangs above the youth and the pulsing urban skyline. While the citizen is immobile, surely dreaming of future urban adventures, the city never sleeps, its urgent rhythms barely contained by its dynamic and mobile architecture.

Villena's narrator, Rafa Antúnez, is shipwrecked in the 1990s. Having succumbed to the lures of capital, he is a commercial screenwriter where once his grand ambition was to be a writer, tout court, the chronicler of an urban life of infinite potential. The careworn Rafa thus exhibits that cessation of interest in the external world and inhibition of the ego which Freud described long ago. However, the lost object is not Francisco Franco, the source of the *mono* for many cultural critics, but rather the movida itself, a time unambiguously described as one of life, liberty, and pleasure. If, as we have seen, urbanism is characterized by colliding temporalities, then this retrospective perspective, persistent throughout the novel, imposes a further level of time-space on the image and experience of Madrid.

Like *La Luna* and *Sólo*, *Madrid ha muerto* can be read as a "choral" or ensemble work: Villena mimes many of the same voices. And, like those earlier works, he combines his praise of the city with a keen sense of irony. But the novel as genre can also be read as a "device" or a "text" that serves to translate social time in ways quite distinct from those of magazines and oral history. For example Villena draws openly and knowingly on a particular literary tradition, the picaresque. His lengthy chapter titles mimic the sententiousness of Guzmán de Alfarache. And while Lazarillo was asked to confess his life story to a archbishop, Rafa is invited to tell his tale by none other than Pedro Almodóvar. There is thus a promiscuous intermingling of real and imaginary characters. Rafa, who claims to be an infrequent contributor to *La Luna*, is given a copy of William Burroughs'

The Wild Boys by the *maudit* Eduardo Haro Ibars (Villena 1999, 80);
seductive Lía, the obscure and ever elusive object of Rafa's desire, is
photographed by Pablo Pérez Mínguez in a studio decorated by
Guillermo Pérez Villalta (*ibid.*, 56). While some of the original *modernos* chose to fictionalize their appearance and experience, adopt-
ing extravagant pseudonyms (Ouka Lele, Fabio McNamara) to
signal that they had become something else in the city, Villena's
counterparts are enveloped in a more generalized fictionality: even
the most seasoned veteran of the movida would have a hard time
distinguishing between real and imaginary, so many and varied are
Madrid ha muerto's characters.

Villena exploits another literary technique familiar from the picaresque: the unreliable narrator. Unlike the journalist and the historian, the novelist and his fictional mouthpiece are freed from the
constraints of accuracy. When "Kostus" is misspelled, who is to
blame? Rafa's chronology is as hazy as his orthography. While he
coincides with *La Luna* and *Sólo* in his choice of two valiant and
lonely pioneers of the *modernos* (Panero and Haro Ibars [Villena
1999, 19]), he gives different versions of his own incorporation into
the movement. Chapter 1 claims it was through an invitation to the
Costus house, followed by the famous Warhol party (*ibid.*, 33, 36).
But chapter 2 begins with the bold assertion that this is a lie ("He
mentido" [*ibid.*, 53]). His first night was in fact another legendary
occasion, when Almodóvar and Fabio played a gig at Rockola (sic).
The fallibility of memory thus merges with the unreliability of narration. But this is not the historical amnesia supposedly typical of
the transition. Rather it is a lapse consistent with cultural geography, according to which which "life histories" are dynamically and
unstably constructed from the intersection of lived time, represented time, and urban space.

Madrid ha muerto thus coincides with the by now loci classici of
the movida: the people, places, and parties are the same as those promoted in the early 1980s by the contributors to *La Luna* and recalled
in the early 1990s by the discussants of *Sólo*. Confirming once more
the intense sociability of the period, the novel is (like its picaresque
models) highly episodic, a parade of drugs, sex, and night life. There
is thus a structural conflict in the novel between linear and circular
time. On the one hand, Villena documents punctual events more or
less in sequence (from the early Warhol party to the late launch of a

book based on the Patti Diphusa column). On the other hand, the endless encounters, both sexual and pharmaceutical, suggest a repetition that is ultimately as wearisome as the social discipline of work. Like the picaresque anti-heroes once more, Rafa barely learns from his experiences and thus seems to be constantly rediscovering themes (such as homosexuality) with which he claims to be unfamiliar.

This breathless social circularity intersects with the slower natural cycle of the seasons. Like *La Luna* and its graphic artist Rodrigo, Villena's narrator is fascinated by summer in the city. The "happiest" time of life and youth, summer suggests particular urban spaces: the terraces on the Castellana (shown in Almodóvar's *La ley del deseo [The Law of Desire]*) and the swimming pools which true madrileños prefer to the sea, and which facilitate the social mixing of working-class toughs and frail transvestites (Villena 1999, 99, 102). The accelerated and protracted beats of the city are thus overlaid with an increasingly insistent annual rhythm that will prove, finally, to be a memento mori.

The classicizing Villena would appreciate another Latin motto here: Et in Arcadia ego. As heroin and AIDS surreptitiously take over the party, so Villena's alter ego (like Pablos in Quevedo's *Buscón*) is co-opted by his master's voice. Villena himself appears intermittently as a character, always ironically undercut. The "vampyric" Haro Ibars complains laughingly that he had to interpret between the affected writer and the urban youths he coveted: Villena "spoke Latin" to them (Villena 1999, 129). But the pallid Rafa, a man without qualities, often takes on the unmistakable tones of Villena himself, both in the eulogies of young male bodies (in spite of his constant insistence on his heterosexuality) and the Wildean paradoxes on life and art. This blurring of narrator and author parallels the blending of past and present produced by the retrospective perspective. But it could also be read sympathetically as testimony to that fluidly festive intermingling, or collective temporality without tradition, that characterized the movida.

Madrid ha muerto ends unambiguously with death and disappointment. Manuel Piña's motto, which gives the novel its title, was spoken when the designer was thrown out of a nightclub for smoking a joint (Villena 1999, 290). Public pleasure is now taboo. Even the party for the Patty Diphusa book (the most lasting cultural survival of *La Luna*) turns into a wake: Almodóvar, when asked, claims that if his heroine were alive today she would be dead (*ibid.*, 276). In Villena's characteristically decadent and pagan style, Madrid has become Thebes, Egyptian city of the dead, and has set off with Anubis on a voyage from which there is no return (*ibid.*, 293). There is a final disavowal here. Like so many movida veterans who have denied the persistence, even existence, of the movement, Villena takes care to remind us, in a final note from the author, that he is not the product of the experience he has described in such luxurious detail ("No soy su hijo" ["I am not its child," *ibid.*, 303]).

There is no doubt, however, of the nature of that experience. It is a freedom that, although lost, is wholly identified with the city: "Madrid había sido la libertad" ("Madrid had meant freedom," Villena 1999, 290). Moreover, the luxury of hindsight allows the narrator to stress the true value of the movida's cultural producers. Where once, shocked by their portrait of Franco's widow, he had thought Costus to be "frivolous," now he recognizes that they were as "hard" and "resistant" as a "rock" (*ibid.*, 35). And unlike other commentators of his age Villena's narrator is not insensitive to the pleasures and places of later neo-tribes. His novel contains a particularly lyrical evocation of an acid-house party fuelled by new drugs (ecstasy), new locations (a field outside the city), new temporal practices (non-stop dancing from night until noon) (*ibid.*, 221). While Rafa himself is "shipwrecked" in the 1990s (*ibid.*, 251), as the Red and Falangist generals were in the 1980s, the transient affinities of urban collectives, indifferent to tradition, are shown to reform elsewhere as soon as they have dissolved.

The time of Madrid

The cultural products I have chosen to analyse (magazine, oral history, and novel) coincide in their insistence on the sheer fun of urban life in democratic Spain. Far from being melancholic they stress the "joviality" of the movida madrileña, contrasting it with the negativity of foreign equivalents such as British punk. Socioeconomic factors for the Spanish state as a whole would appear to confirm that intuition through the 1980s. The full statistical analysis in Carlos Alonso Zaldívar and Manuel Castells' *España, fin de siglo* (1992) shows that unemployment remained shockingly high. However, other negative indicators, such as divorce and births out of wedlock, remained well below the European median. Contrary to stereotype, electoral abstention did not increase over time (*ibid.*, 29). From 1984 to 1989 an increasing majority of Spaniards expressed themselves "satisfied" with their democracy, reaching rates above those of neighbouring countries with much longer established democratic governance. Moreover, as the decade progressed Spaniards were more and more convinced that they now enjoyed greater freedom than under the dictatorship and that "democracy is always the best system of government" (*ibid.*, 30). Empirical indicators of social attitudes thus tend to support neither the "mourning and melancholia" hypothesis of pathological grief nor the "spectacle and simulacrum" theory of irresponsible and apolitical hedonism.

One area where there does indeed seem to be a kind of amnesia is the lack of reference to women's contribution to the movida. Unfortunately this absence is characteristic of the primary sources I treat here, all authored by men. However even this gap is now starting to be filled. Chus Gutiérrez' feature film *El Calentito* (2005), named for a fictional nightclub clearly modelled on Rock-Ola, is the first full scale cinematic recreation of the period. It is one that focuses overwhelmingly and for the first time on women's cultural creativity: an all-girl punk group put on a triumphant performance on the night of the attempted coup by Tejero, the so-called 23-F. Period footage from Almodóvar's *Laberinto de pasiones* (*Labyrinth of Passion*, 1982) mingles with Gutiérrez's expert reconstruction.

The movida had its victims. But it is not clear that they were more numerous than those of earlier subcultures which had the considerable good fortune to precede the emergence of AIDS. The movida produced no bloody drama comparable to the shooting of Warhol in the Factory or the murder-suicide of Sid and Nancy in the Chelsea Hotel. Nor did these comparable Anglo-American subcultures produce a luminary as durably productive and successful as Almodóvar. Even a figure as fragile and evanescent as Fabio McNamara, who did not achieve the fame he craved, managed to cheat death. On 7 June 2005 Rodrigo, invisible for twenty years, reappeared at the opening of an exhibition of his work at Madrid's Sins Entido (sic) gallery. The focus of the retrospective was the long lost *Manuel*, now reclaimed for the capital's first festival of LGBT arts. Other contributors to *La Luna* continue to make substantial but unshowy careers in contemporary Spanish art, design, music, and literature.

There is no shame or surprise in the fact that the movement, if such it was, did not last for ever. As we have seen, neo-tribes are transient. Durable cultural vitality is as difficult to procure as urban harmony. Indeed both are probably utopian, as art and the city are not things but processes whose ends are impossible to predict. What I have suggested, however, is that we replace the psychoanalytic model of persistent, unexorcised trauma with a more sympathetic geographical model which relates cultural products to the time-space complex of daily life, dense as it is with velocities, directions, turnings, and detours. Such a model prizes the freedom and lack of inhibition characteristic of the texts I have studied.

In one frame of Rodrigo's *Manuel*, the beloved's black, bedroom eyes are made to rhyme with the street lamps that halo his head (*La Luna* no. 2, December 1983). Throughout *La Luna*, *Sólo*, and *Madrid ha muerto*, the erotic flow of the city is felt to be as intense, ubiquitous, and immaterial as electricity. The challenge for readers and viewers is to respond to this invitation to pleasure without abandoning critical judgement. I have suggested, however, that this pleasure is no mere thoughtless hedonism. The urban pedagogy expressed by these cultural producers, none of whom was well paid for their labour, can be read as a cultural good that supplements formal democratic structures. Even Villena claims, ironically, that those who were so generous in sharing their beds with others should be granted the status of a non-government organisation (Villena 1999, 277). The final gift of this social and sociable economy, then, is that, aggressively rooted as it is, it can still help to "break down intractable localness" and "transcend the limitations of place" (Amin, Cameron, and Hudson 2002, 115). If the "time of Madrid" hymned by *La Luna* has passed (and this is by no means certain) then surely we should celebrate the heritage it has left behind.

Works cited

Amin, Ash, Cameron, Angus and Hudson, Ray. *Placing the Social Economy*. London and New York: Routledge, 2002.

Amin, Ash, Massey, Doreen and Thrift, Nigel. *Cities for the Many, Not for the Few*. Bristol: Policy, 2000.

Castilla, Toñeta. 'Cerrojos y polvo: la mayor parte de "los templos" de la movida han sido clausurados o han cambiado de actividad.' *El País* [Madrid] 11 May 1994, 7.

Crang, Mike. 'Rhythms of the city: temporalized space and motion.' In May and Thrift (2001), 187–207.

Freud, Sigmund. 'Mourning and melancholia.' In *On Metapsychology*. London: Penguin, 1991, 251–68.

Gallero, José Luis. *Sólo se vive una vez: esplendor y ruina de la movida madrileña*. Madrid: Ardora, 1991.

La Luna de Madrid 1–26 (November 1983–March 1986).

Loureiro, Angel. Unpublished paper read at conference 'In Living Culture: The Place of Emotions in the Americas and Beyond.' Yale University, 11–12 April 2003.

May, Jon and Thrift, Nigel (eds), *TimeSpace: Geographies of Temporality*. London: Routledge, 2001.

Medina Domínguez, Alberto. *Exorcismos de la memoria: políticas y poéticas de la melancolía en la España de la transición*. Madrid: Libertarias, 2001.

Moreiras Menor, Cristina. *Cultura herida: literatura y cine en la España democrática*. Madrid: Libertarias, 2002.

Savage, Jon. *England's Dreaming*. Second edition. New York: St Martin's, 2002.

Stein, Jean and Plimpton, George. *Edie: An American Biography*. New York: Random House, 1984.

Thrift, Nigel. *Spatial Formations*. London: Sage, 1996.

Vattimo, Gianni. *The End of Modernity*. Cambridge: Polity, 1988.

Vilarós, Teresa M. *El mono del desencanto: una crítica cultural de la transición española (1973–93)*. Madrid: Siglo XXI, 1998.

Villena, Luis Antonio de. *Madrid ha muerto: esplendor y caos en una ciudad feliz de los ochenta*. Barcelona: Planeta, 1999.

Zaldívar, Carlos Alonso and Castells, Manuel. *España, fin de siglo*. Madrid: Alianza, 1992.

Towards the Spanish youth movie: **4**
Historias del Kronen

Visible youth

The youth movie would seem to be about anything but youth. In a recent paper on Argentine youth movies from the 1960s to the 1990s Laura Podalsky (2003) argues that the category "youth" stands in for a crisis in the public sphere and is constituted by multiple discourses (such as legal and psychological) and multiple institutions (such as education and the police). Moreover there is a historical development. While earlier films followed a Bildungsroman format and had their teenage tearaways finally tamed by social integration, more recent films are "depoliticized," a tendency attacked by both Right and Left. Politically ambivalent, the youth movie is thus also historically complex: the representation of contemporary society to itself, it is also (and paradoxically) the "legacy of the past," a peculiarly intense marker of social change.

Since they emerged in the US in the 1950s youth or teen movies have, then, carried this double burden of authenticity (correspondence to the real) and ambivalence (the tension between nihilism and redemption). Indeed the unfocused nature of teen angst is proclaimed from the very start of the genre. James Dean's rebel is without a cause; Marlon Brando's *Wild One* famously responds to the question "What are you rebelling against?" with a defiant "What've you got?"

How, then, does this paradigm translate to the very different circumstances of twentieth-century Spain? While little research has been done on the topic, there is an excellent collection of essays which gives an overview of the field (Cueto 1998). Significantly the subjects, who in English might be called "juvenile delinquents," are named "desarraigados" or "the uprooted," implying a fixity of origin or location that has been violently terminated. The authors trace a broad movement in Spanish film from the "non-existent reality" of marginalized youth in the moralizing 1950s, via the *pijos* and *ye-yés* (rich kids and groovy teens) of the developing 1960s to the urban hoodlums and knife fighters of the 1970s and 1980s. For the alien-ated youth of the 1990s, we are told there were "neither rebels, nor causes" (*ibid.*, 113). Interestingly, however, and as in the case of Argentina, elements of the earlier films are repeated in the most recent ones. Youthful delinquents of the 1950s are generally *niños bien* (children of "good family"); the exclusion of women from the genre is reinforced in the 1970s and 1980s when Eloy de la Iglesia's male hooligans are presented in an overtly homoerotic manner. As we shall see, *Historias del Kronen* (the best known youth movie of the 1990s) continues these lines by basing its episodic narrative of juve-nile misadventures in Madrid on the unknowledged love or lust of one wealthy teen for another.

In his account of the 1990s in *Los desarraigados* Jesús Palacios (1998) begins by arguing that the terms "youth" and "Spanish cinema" are mutually exclusive, in spite of the fact that "youthful-ness" is the trademark of Spanish film in that decade (Cueto 1998, 113). He describes *Historias del Kronen* as the "phenomenon" of the 1990s, the most characteristic expression of this trend (*ibid.*, 120). Curiously, however, *Kronen*'s production was marked by tension. In an interview in the same volume grizzled middle-aged director Montxo Armendáriz openly admits his lack of sympathy for both the characters and narrative; and he recounts an argument with José Angel Mañas, the youthful and photogenic author of the novel on which his film was based (*ibid.*, 156). The latter stopped coming to the set because of disagreements over the apparently trivial matter of his young rebels' wardrobe. Coinciding perhaps with Palacios' view that youth is an unaccustomed or unwelcome subject in Spanish film, Armendáriz notes that *Kronen* was released around the same time as US and French youth movies which enjoyed much greater success abroad (*ibid.*, 157).

The best known historian of contemporary Spanish film also dis-misses youth movies as a "sub-genre" in his survey of the 1990s (Heredero 2002, 75). Yet he manages to list no fewer than twenty-six titles that appeared in Spain during the decade, many of them like *Kronen* both popular and critical successes. Interestingly the social context for this increased cinematic visibility is ambivalent. Jesús M. de Miguel writes of a new academic interest in youth by sociologists in the early 1990s (1998, 52), coinciding with a con-tinued insistence by conservative Catholics on the supposed lack of

moral values exhibited by young Spaniards (*ibid.*, 253). Writings by
the revolutionary youth movements that immediately followed the
death of Franco in 1975 argue for an increased participation in society and politics by a marginalized youth which, with the coming of
democracy, would rapidly renounce such ambitions. In one such
radical volume the youthful authors (Reguant and Castillejo 1976)
cite cinema as both a valuable place for young people to hang out
and a stultifying way for teens to kill time: they discover that most of
the young patrons lining up for a showing have not even taken the
trouble to find out which film is showing in the single screen theatres
of the day (*ibid.*, 126). We shall see in a moment that the demography of cinema audiences is also a source of tension for Spanish
youth movies.

Mark Allinson stresses the "internationalism" of young
Spaniards in the 1990s: consumerist, pragmatic, and apolitical
(2000, 271). It remains the case, however, that the extreme com-
modification of youth in the US revealed in surveys such as Alissa
Quart's *Branded: The Buying and Selling of Teenagers* (2003) is
unknown in Spain. We need only compare Quart's lavishly catered
Bar Mitzvahs and Quinceañeras with *Kronen*'s raucous but improvised birthday party. And in his study of *Historias del Kronen*, both
novel and film, Santiago Fouz-Hernández (2000) has shown that
the term "Generation X," which arose in the US and was freely
applied to contemporary Spanish youth by local commentators,
refers to quite different cultural expressions in France, the UK, the
US, and Spain. While there is in all these countries (in mid-1990s
films such as *La Haine, Trainspotting, Kids,* and *Kronen*) a sense of
generalized loss and confusion at the fin de siècle, the intersection
of the category of youth with other factors such as race, sex, class,
and violence is clearly distinct or "territorialized" in each country
(*ibid.*, 95).

In Spain there is a particular irony that the vogue for cinematic
youth should have arisen during a decade when the Spanish birth
rate fell to amongst the lowest in the world. As William Chislett
writes, this decline in fertility meant a rapid acceleration in aging
in the Spanish population as a whole (2002, 29). Not for the first
time, film was out of step with social change. Demography is, of
course, also vital for the film industry. Where youth movies in the
US have been sustained by the continued dominance of the teenage

demographic in North American movie theatres, the situation in Spain is more complex. A recent survey of cultural habits by Spanish producers discovered that the cinema audience is indeed youthful, that interest in filmgoing falls off with increasing age, and that movies are part of "youth culture" (SGAE 2000, 77, 78). However, while over 35s rarely venture out to the cinema, the "core" audience of those aged 21–24 is slightly older than in the US and is defined as upper-middle-class, university educated, and urban, even "elitist" (*ibid.*, 72, 73, 74). Moreover Hollywood films are preferred by Spaniards who are very young (under 20) and with only a high school diploma; Spanish films are the choice of older audiences and those who have benefited from further education (*ibid.*, 84). And while US "event movies" attract young people through their high concept themes, Spanish features appeal to an older and more educated audience who are familiar with their actors and directors (*ibid.*, 89, 92). The popular success of *Historias del Kronen*, then, its ability to serve as the cultural "phenomenon" of the 1990s, were thus by no means assured. A Spanish youth movie could not rely on the good will of a youthful audience more enamoured of Hollywood; and the educated and older demographic who favoured local films would require convincing (like the director himself) that this theme was one with which they could sympathize or empathize.

Released on 28 April 1995, *Kronen* took 2.3 million euros and was seen by 771,950 Spaniards (Ministerio de Cultura), thus figuring amongst the top five grossing domestic movies of the year, even at a time when Spanish cinema was experiencing one of its periodic renaissances. It also won the Goya (Spanish Oscar) for best adapted screenplay. The secret of *Kronen*'s success lies perhaps in its distribution and the care with which it was presented to a diverse public. The notes (Renoir 1996) given out in the lobbies of the Renoir art house chain in Madrid (a vital forum for exhibition) begin with a bio of *Kronen*'s veteran producer, Elías Querejeta, a distinguished figure still haloed by his association with classic works by Saura and Erice some twenty years earlier. Querejeta is a specialist, we are told, in *cine de autor* ("auteur cinema"). Only subsequently are we given of the director's record in making films on *jóvenes desarraigados* ("rootless youth"). But the titles chosen are impeccably progressive and calculated to appeal to an older educated audience: *Tasio* (period Basque rural drama) and *Las cartas de Alou* (*Letters from Alou*, contemporary melodrama on immigration). Much more typical of Armendáriz than the urban *Kronen* will be his yet more successful rural coming of age drama, *Secretos del corazón* (*Secrets of the Heart*, 1997), a project which he tells us in the published script drew on his innermost personal experience (Armendáriz 2000, 5). Meanwhile the only established actor in *Kronen*'s young cast, Jordi Mollà, was known for his difficulty, even intellectualism. A typical cover feature in film magazine *Cinemanía* describes him as private and elusive (M.C. 1998); for Chris Perriam he embodies a "troubled masculinity" (2003, 127). It thus follows that the public images of producer, director, and actor coincided in providing an initial impression of artistic "quality" at odds with the commercialism with which the youth movie was commonly associated in both Spain and the US.

Press coverage confirms the ambivalence inherent in the project of a youth movie made by and, to some extent for, discerning adults. The most prestigious daily writes that *Kronen* is an "exemplary film" precisely because it transcends the specificity of its milieu (*niños pijos madrileños* ["rich kids in Madrid"]) to address "permanent questions of life in any place and time" (Fernández-Santos 1995). This view of the timelessness of the picture coincides with that of the director who repeatedly claims in interview that "youth has always and will always be transgressive" (e.g. Gil 1995). Conversely a rival paper writes that *Kronen* is representative of a new trend in Spanish cinema: "bad films well made" (Marías 1998). While technically the film is "irreproachable," it is an example of manipulative commercialism, a would-be "auteur movie" sabotaged by inauthenticity. Critical controversy was echoed by the audience. Two weeks after *Kronen* opened, *El País* interviewed spectators as they emerged from a screening (Jarque 1995). Interestingly they belonged to all age groups. Older viewers, attracted by media coverage, disliked the film on the grounds of its inauthenticity and immorality, claiming it gave an "erroneous view" of youth and yet might inspire copycat violence. Even teenage girls who volunteered that "things are like [the film shows]," confessed they did not identify with *Kronen*'s characters. Young women (marginalized in the film itself) were perhaps attracted to its audience by photo spreads in the glossies which had focused since preproduction on creating a new star in the attractive figure of Juan Diego Botto, who was to play protagonist Carlos. (Botto would be duly rewarded with a Goya nomination for best new actor.) Smooth skinned and floppy haired, a cigarette dangling provocatively from his sensual lips, he is interviewed in one magazine surrounded by buzz words and quotes from the novel ("the emblematic book of the Spanish Generation X"): "sex," "violence," "money," "alcohol" (López 1994). In *Kronen*'s coverage in the print media, then, timelessness is juxtaposed with contemporaneity, auteurism with sensationalism.

Academic interpretations, when they came, were equally diverse, thus suggesting that *Kronen* was an unusually rich text. Gonzalo Navajas (2002) had placed the novel within a nihilistic version of postmodernism: *Kronen*, he claims, bears witness to a time in which there is no consciousness, no depth, and no grand narrative beyond individualism, a time when abstract or absolute values are exiled to the past (95). Cristina Moreiras-Menor's (2002) reading is equally broad. *Kronen*, both novel and film, testifies to the consumerist horror of the 1990s, a traumatic experience in which public space is exhausted (*ibid.*, 206) and private space invaded by television (*ibid.*, 211). Pilar Rodríguez (2002) also cites the "void and volence" of 1990s youth (175), but particularizes them by referring to the "generational conflict" between director Armendáriz and author Mañas (*ibid.*, 181) and to more precise social changes in Spain: the decline of the welfare state; the crisis in patriarchal society; youth consumerism; international youth mass media; and the erosion of residual moral Puritanism (*ibid.*, 180–1; see also Ballesteros 2002). Like other commentators, she also notes the softening of tone from novel to film: Armendáriz not only reduces the original's racism and sexism, he also provides a possibility of redemption at the end of the film, a possibility rejected by the novel's defiant nihilism (Rodríguez 2002, 188).

It is constructive to contrast journalistic and academic responses to those of contemporary consumers in Spain. Amateur reviews on websites tell a rather different story. While many young viewers contribute to the inconclusive authenticity/inauthenticity debate (i.e. whether or not "things are really like that"), others show a keen awareness of the particularity of the film's social and historical context. One hostile reviewer calculates the (to him implausible) cost of the aimless, leisured lifestyle enjoyed by the film's teens (Vainsteins 2001). Another waxes nostalgic on the technological innocence of the mid 1990s as shown in the film, a time when satellite TV and mobile telephony were in their infancy: surely that was a golden age of sociability, when kids, unburdened by technology, wanted to live life more fully and spend more time with friends (Fronteramix 2001). However unconvincing this reading is, its awareness of recent changes in communication technology contrasts with the broad brush of academics such as Moreiras-Menor (2002) for whom *Kronen* testifies to the complete collapse of a private space invaded by mass media.

A third young consumer (Ivana 2000) proves to be aware of the packaging of what was then a new generation of young performers who had yet to prove themselves to local audiences, an aspect ignored by Olympian reviewers such as Fernández-Santos (1995). It seems clear, then, that media-savvy younger spectators are more conscious of and responsive to details of mise en scène (such as phones) which remain invisible to older critics and scholars. It seems appropriate, therefore, that the "generational conflict" between director and author (who collaborated on the script) should have been fought in part over the wardrobe: while Armendáriz deliberately avoided fashionable garments, claiming they would soon look dated, Mañas knew that the perceived authenticity of the film would depend on such details. Indeed where the film is studiously anonymous in its use of commodities (with the exception of the beer whose abbreviated name gives it its title), the novel is littered with brand names, phonetically transcribed into Spanish.

A sense of spatiality

Most viewers today will experience *Kronen* through a medium little known at the time of its theatrical release: DVD. The synopsis on the back of the disc remains the same as the one used in press and promotional materials on the film's theatrical release:

Carlos es un joven estudiante que apenas ha cumplido 21 años. Como cada día, al atardecer, sale de su casa para reunirse con sus amigos del Kronen, el bar que más frecuentan. Es verano, Carlos está de vacaciones. Vive de noche. Cualquier situación puede llevarse un poco más lejos.

Ningún límite es admitido, ninguna barrera aceptada. Y cada vez más, una aventura se encadena con otra como si se tratara de una noche continuada, con la voluntad de vivir cada instante como si fuera el último. Sin embargo, algo de lo que ocurre sitúa a Carlos y a su cuadrilla frente a una realidad que han intentado ignorar hasta ese momento ...

Carlos is a young student who is barely 21. Every evening he leaves home to meet his friends in the Kronen, their favourite bar. It is summer and Carlos is on holiday. He lives at night. Any situation can go a bit too far. There are no limits, no boundaries. And more and more one adventure leads to another as if there was just one long night and the desire to live each moment as if it was the last. However, something happens that sets Carlos and his gang up against a reality they have tried to ignore until now ...

Like Spanish press reviews, the synopsis is strangely abstract. It fails even to name the location or the name of any character beyond Carlos, the nominal protagonist of this ensemble picture. The reality the friends have sought to ignore remains unclear: is it the general fin de siècle or postmodern malaise cited by critics, the more particular homoerotic desire of Mollà's closeted Roberto for his attractive and abusive "best friend" Carlos, or the very precise murder at a climactic party of Aitor Merino's Pedro, a sickly, effeminate sidekick?

The twelve chapters into which the DVD is divided provide an alternative approach to the narrative. They suggest not only the episodic structure so typical of the youth movie but also the dependence of the film on concrete locations or, to put it more technically, on the spatialization of character and action. "Inicio" ("Beginning") establishes Carlos in his chosen habitat of the bar. "La ruta" ("The road") follows the gang in their car to another urban space, the dance hall. "Manãna no existe" ("Tomorrow doesn't exist") has the boys taunting a prostitute by a park and robbing a convenience store. "Vacaciones" ("Holidays") shows us Carlos's uneasy existence in his parents' upper-middle-class home, complete with maid. With "El aniversario" ("The Anniversary") Carlos accompanies his mild mannered sister to a restaurant with their parents, while in "El abuelo" he visits his dying grandfather, who laments the nihilism of contemporary life, so different to the politically engaged past he remembers. "El puente" ("The bridge") marks the site where the fragile Pedro is challenged to a macho trial by an anonymous hunk (future star Eduardo Noriega in his first role): hanging precariously above the streaming traffic of an urban highway. In "Sigue la noche" ("The night goes on") the boys attend a rock concert by one of their number, while in "La piscina" ("The swimming pool") the central couple go skinny dipping in a deserted suburban pool (the rare frontal male nudity is reminiscent of Eloy de la Iglesia's homoerotic heroes some twenty years earlier). "El entierro" ("The funeral") requires Carlos to visit the cemetery, "La fiesta" ("The party"), the family home of Pedro. Finally in "Muerte y desenlace" ("Death and conclusion"), the murder leads to a trip to the hospital and Carlos and Roberto's concluding struggle over a videotape which provides evidence of both the brutal murder and an equally abrupt and ill fated sexual encounter between the two leads.

Kronen, then, is episodic in narrative and impoverished in characterization. But it is rich in locations which compensate for the absence of other aspects of feature film production. After all the very title tells us that these are stories not of people but of a place. Technically the places shown are "third spaces" (i.e. neither work nor home). Some (the bar and dance hall) are intended for juvenile use. Others are more typically appropriated by the young men: the pool is normally frequented by families; the bridge is intended for crossing not hanging; the city street itself is diverted from pure circulation of traffic to a new festive and perilous use as an impromptu race track. The final party location is a bourgeois home overtaken by dangerous, even deadly, play in the absence of its owners. This sense of spatiality (of the primacy of location over character and plot) is echoed in publicity materials for the film. The two images used for the poster and DVD cover, and frequently reproduced in the press, are an exterior of the two youths hanging from the bridge, suspended over speeding cars; and an interior of the dance hall with a young performer supported on the raised arms of the audience. Both pictures feature minor characters whose faces are hidden from view. One generic punk song on the soundtrack repeats the refrain: "No hay sitio para ti" ("There's no place for you"). However, the film is based precisely on a repeated and failed attempt to appropriate space, to reconcile the body and the city, each as anonymous as the other.

Let us look closely at two sequences to see how this works in practice. The film opens with stark credits (white on a black screen) set not to music but to sounds of the city: trains, traffic, and pneumatic drills. The camera pans slowly from left to right from a high viewpoint over the anonymous cityscape in late afternoon, coming to rest on an urban highway that only residents will recognize as the M-30, a significant location in both novel and film. There is a dissolve to another high angle shot, this time static, of the Manhattan-like towers of Azca at dusk, glowing in the dark. Locals, once more, will recognize one steel and glass tower as the Torre Picasso, the highest inhabited building in Madrid. Beside it, the great artery of the Castellana glows red and silver with streaming cars. The soundtrack now features ringing phones and station announcements. We cut to an anonymous city street at ground level and at night. The camera moves out from behind a parked car and tracks forward behind a youth in medium shot (shiny black hair, striped T-shirt, and tight blue jeans). He stands out in front of the plain façade of a bar: the sign *Cervecería Kronen* glows dully in red as punk music sounds low on the soundtrack. Armendáriz twice cuts briefly back to the urban landscape before the camera finally moves inside the bar to show Juan Diego Botto's Carlos from the front. Handsome and self-assured, he cops a free beer from the barman, Manolo (who will prove to be a regular of his gang), before making his way to a table at the back where his friends are already sitting. Roberto (Jordi Mollà), visibly older and wearing a red T-shirt that rhymes with that of Carlos) stands out screen left: the others are reduced to the background. Carlos playfully (provocatively) pokes Roberto in the ribs and slaps his cheek, and Roberto teases him in turn about his absent girlfriend (Figure 9). Mollà sends Botto a significant look: the attentive viewer already sees that there is something more than masculine horseplay between them. The implicit homoeroticism of the youth movie will become finally, brutally explicit by the time *Kronen* is over.

The opening cityscapes could be read simply as establishing shots, creating a context for the action to come. But crosscut as they are with Carlos's entry into the bar they suggest rather a certain crisis in the public sphere typical of the youth movie, an attempt to integrate modern city and youthful body. Indeed it is no accident that the camera should dwell on the Torre Picasso, which one guide book of the 1990s tells us was designed by the same architect as New York's ill fated World Trade Center and embodies the "modernity" of the capital (Anaya 1991, 13). The soundtrack here, apparently random, introduces those legal and institutional discourses such as that of the police which define "modern youth" as a troubled category, and whose absence will lead to tragedy. Although the streets and buildings may prove difficult to locate by non-native viewers (Armendáriz omits more distinctive historical buildings), they still serve as a sign of contemporaneity that underwrites the authenticity of the narrative to come, appealing as they do to the familiar trope of urban alienation. Crucially, however, there is no contact between this general overview (the privileged perspective of the city seen from on high) and the particular experience (the limited viewpoint of the young man briefly stalking the city street and haunting its bars).

Carlos, then, is initially as anonymous as the city itself, pointedly shown from behind. But this opening sequence serves both to establish Botto as a new star (abandoning the bird's eye view, we will see only from his viewpoint) and to introduce us to a "new generation" of actors in crowded group shots. But the more experienced Mollà already stands out, with an actorly performance suggesting from the very beginning an ambivalent range of emotions: desire, distrust, fear, and envy. The director's technique, on the other hand, is unremarkable. There is nothing in the shooting or cutting style that draws attention to itself. For example, conversation is shown conventionally in shot/reverse shot (ie cutting between Carlos's and Roberto's point of view). The mise en scène is equally unremarkable. The flat lighting in the bar comes from ugly fluorescents. The wardrobe and soundtrack are strangely unstylish for wealthy youths (*niños bien* or *pijos*) who might be expected to have an interest in fashion and music. (One of Carlos' later costumes, a 1980s-style stripy shirt, makes him look more like a vacationing stockbroker than a teenager.) *Kronen* could not be further from flashy foreign rivals like *La Haine* with its luscious black and white photography, virtuoso camerawork, and charismatic multiracial cast. But Armendáriz's film is also distinct from Mañas' novel, which shows a surer grasp of teenage taste of the period: the film's generic punk and heavy metal is eclipsed by the novel's precise and knowing references to British indie rock (The The), Seattle grunge

(Nirvana), and the Spanish electronic dance music known as *bakalao*. In this question of cultural taste or distinction, there is thus a certain tension between contemporaneity and timelessness, or, to put it in spatial terms, location and dislocation. Interestingly, the Basque director also omits Carlos' frequent references to the "hatred" for the central capital of Madrid felt by the unwilling Spanish citizens of the periphery (e.g. Mañas 1999, 11). The film is thus cut loose (indeed, uprooted) from the precise cultural and political context of the novel, which many potential viewers might find obscure (varieties of popular music) or unsavoury (attacks on the "historic nationalities").

As critics have noted (e.g. Rodríguez 2002, 187–8)), the film diverges most clearly from the novel at the end. "La fiesta" ("The party," chapter 11 of the DVD) begins with an extreme closeup of Carlos's fingers dialling on a land line phone, the kind of detail which, as we have seen, contemporary teen viewers are quick to spot. This time his long suffering girlfriend refuses to talk to him. Carlos then eavesdrops as his mother sacks the maid for stealing money that he himself has taken. Any sympathy we may feel for his character is thus compromised, as ever, by evidence of his continuing immoralism. The audience remains ambivalent. Later sickly Pedro greets the gang at the door of his absent parents' home holding a camcorder, another detail of technological consumerism. Here however it will serve as an appropriate equivalent for a novelistic technique used in the original. Where Mañas sets this scene apart typographically and perspectivally (in a novel of multivoiced dialogue we are for once given only Carlos' words), Armendáriz shoots the party through the "subjective" camcorder in a technically impressive unbroken take that lasts a full five minutes. Performance style, driven perhaps by the unusual demands of this sequence shot, becomes increasingly showy also: Mollà's dancing here, a frenzy of jerking limbs and desperate looks, signals "troubled masculinity" with a vengeance.

Homoeroticism also comes to the fore when Carlos dances wildly and mockingly with Pedro (who has been constantly taunted for his effeminacy), before following Roberto out to the garden where they voyeuristically watch a straight couple having sex. The camera, previously passed from hand to hand, now comes to rest on the floor as Carlos lunges for Roberto's crotch and (just out of shot) gives him a brutally brief hand job. When Roberto then tries to kiss Carlos his rejection is equally brutal. Carlos goes on to tie and torture Pedro, forcing him to drink a bottle of whisky which he knows will kill him (Figure 10). All this is shown, once more, through the camcorder, left running on the floor.

The sequence is clearly sensationalist, condensing as it does three of the buzz words exploited in the film's prepublicity: "sex," "violence," and "alcohol." Yet the showy camera technique, unique in the film, also reinforces *Kronen*'s auteurist quality or artistic distinction at this crucial point. Moreover the intensity of the violence, also unique in the film, contrasts with the unusual domesticity of the mise en scène. Unlike the rather bleak space of the bar, this is a comfortable, even welcoming setting, with plush furniture and bourgeois knick-knacks (a silver horse sits on the mantelpiece). Proving once more the primacy of location in *Kronen*, the appropriation of this space signals the annihilation of the weakest character and the climactic point of the action.

After speeding with the dying Pedro to the hospital (as before they had raced through the streets for fun), Carlos and Roberto return to watch the incriminating videotape. Where previously they watched *Henry, Diary of a Serial Killer* with practised and morbid delight, now their eyes grow damp with tears at this real-life snuff movie. Taking a moral stand, Carlos says the tape must be shown to the authorities. Taunting Roberto a final time for being unable to admit his homosexuality, Carlos struggles with him for the tape. Their fight, like their earlier lovemaking, is just out of shot. The film ends with a closeup of a broken mirror, a clear sign of a rupture in representation. The ideological ambivalence of the film hitherto is now resolved as Carlos takes up an ethical, if not political, position for the very first time.

Unlike *Kronen* the novel (where an indifferent Carlos escapes to the seaside after the murder), *Kronen* the film can thus be read as a Bildungsroman reminiscent of the 1950s youth movie: the nihilism trumpeted so much in the film's "Generation X" publicity materials is finally trumped by redemption. It is perhaps no accident that the "making of" documentary on *Kronen*'s DVD is bookended by scenes from *Rebel Without a Cause*, in which James Dean also learns a lesson about love and death. While Carlos' conversion is hardly enough to satisfy Catholic moralists convinced of the sinfulness of contemporary Spanish youth, it is surely sufficient to reconcile an older, progressive filmmaker such as Armendáriz to the excesses of *niños bien*, even if it failed to convince the mature and educated target audience who favour Spanish films at home. Certainly *Kronen* inserts the young protagonists once more into the institutional discourse of the police (to whom we assume Carlos will hand the tape). Ironically it does so through that very consumerist technology (in this case, the camcorder) which some academic commentators have accused of abolishing, postmodern-style, all possibility of social action. Armendáriz had already taken care, again unlike the novel, to suggest that Carlos does indeed have some measure of self-consciousness and introspection: during his visit to the grandfather he shows signs of sympathy, even sentimentality. But the softening of Manãs' hard-edged conclusion reveals the true legacy of the past implicit in Armendáriz's valiant but failed attempt at a Spanish youth movie. Rather than being about itself, youth once more stands in for something else: that crisis in the public sphere which for a nostalgic older generation can be resolved only by a personal commitment to social responsibility.

Works cited

Allinson, Mark. 'The construction of youth in Spain in the 1980s and 1990s.' In Barry Jordan and Rikki Morgan-Tamosunas (eds), *Contemporary Spanish Cultural Studies*. London: Arnold, 2000, 264–73.

Anaya. *Guía de Madrid hoy*. Madrid: Grupo Anaya, 1991.

Armendáriz, Montxo. *Secretos del corazón: guión cinematográfico*. Madrid: Espiral, 2000.

Ballesteros, Isolina. *Cine (in)surgente: Textos fílmicos y contextos culturales de la España postfranquista*. Madrid: Fundamentos, 2002.

Chislett, William. *The Internationalization of the Spanish Economy*. Madrid: Real Instituto Elcano, 2002.

Cueto, Roberto (ed.). *Los desarraigados en el cine español*. Gijón: Festival Internacional de Cine, 1998.

de Miguel, Jesús M. *Estructura y cambio social en España*. Madrid: Alianza, 1998.

Fernández-Santos, Angel. 'Una película ejemplar.' [review of *Historias del Kronen*] *El País: Espectáculos* 30 April 1995, 31.

Fouz-Hernández, Santiago. '¿Generación X? Spanish urban youth culture at the end of the century in Mañas's/Armendáriz's *Historias del Kronen*.' *Romance Studies* 18.1, 2000, 83–98.

Gil, Cristina. 'Montxo Armendáriz estrena el viernes "Los chicos del Kronen" [sic].' *Ya: Espectáculos* 27 April 1995, 58.

Heredero, Carlos. *Semillas de futuro: cine español 1990–2001*. Madrid: Nuevo Milenio, 2002.

Jarque, Fietta. 'Controversia entre el público.' *El País: Cultura* 12 May 1995, 38.

López, M. J. 'El asesino del Kronen comienza a actuar.' *El País de las Tentaciones: Cine* 19 August 1994, 10–13.

Mañas, José Angel. *Historias del Kronen*. Barcelona: Destino, 1999.

Marías, Miguel. 'Malos filmes bien hechos.' *El Mundo: La Esfera* 7 September 1996, iv.

M. C. 'Jordi Mollà.' *Cinemanía* September 1998, 13.

Moreiras-Menor, Cristina. *Cultura herida: literatura y cine en la España democrática*. Madrid: Libertarias, 2002.

Navajas, Gonzalo. *La narrativa española en la era global*. Barcelona: EUB, 2002.

Palacios, Jesús. 'Ni rebeldes, ni causa: los años 90.' In Cueto (1998), 113–40.

Perriam, Chris. *Stars and Masculinities in Spanish Cinema*. Oxford: Oxford University Press, 2003.

Podalsky, Laura. 'Coming of age: film, affect, and the public sphere.' Paper read at XXIV International Congress of the Latin American Studies Association, Dallas, 27 March 2003.

Quart, Alissa. *Branded: The Buying and Selling of Teenagers*. London: Arrow, 2003.

Reguant, Francesc and Castillejo, Germán. *Juventud y democracia: crónicas del movimiento juvenil*. Barcelona: Avance, 1976.

Renoir. *Historias del Kronen* [cinema lobby notes]. Madrid: Renoir, 1996.

Rodríguez, María Pilar. *Mundos en conflicto: aproximaciones al cine vasco de los noventa*. San Sebastián: Universidad de Deusto, 2002.

SGAE. *Informe sobre hábitos de consumo cultural*. Madrid: SGAE, 2000.

Electronic sources

Fronteramix. '*Historias del Kronen*: cualquier parecido con la reali-
   dad es pura coincidencia.' 20 November 2001. Accessed 5
   August 2003. www.dooyoo.es
Ivana. '*Historias del Kronen*: muy amena y divertida.' 30 July 2000.
   Accessed 5 August 2003. www.dooyoo.es
Ministerio de Cultura. Accessed 5 August 2003. www.mcu.es
Vainsteins. '*Historias del Kronen*: marca la generación de los 90.'
   11 June 2001. Accessed 5 August 2003. www.dooyoo.es

1   Benigno (Javier Cámara) at the window. Pedro Almodóvar,
    Hable con ella (*Talk to Her*, 2002).

2   Marco (Dario Grandinetti) and Benigno merge in reflection. *Hable con ella*.

3   The Alcántaras watch TV, left to right: father Antonio (Imanol Arias),
    mother Merche (Ana Duato), child Carlitos (Ricardo Gómez),
    grandmother (María Galiana). Televisión Española, *Cuéntame cómo
    pasó* (*Tell Me How It Happened*, 2001–).

4 In the suburban kitchen, Nacho (Emilio Aragón) and extended family. Tele 5, *Médico de familia* (*Family Doctor*, 1995–99).

5 In the urban bar, left to right: Diana (Anabel Alonso), Aída (Carmen Machi), and Sole (Amparo Baró). Tele 5, *7 Vidas* (*Seven* or *Nine Lives*, 1999–).

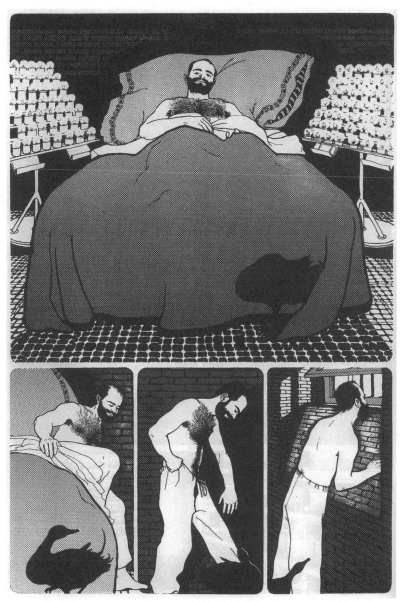

6 Waking up. Rodrigo, *Manuel* (graphic novel published in *La Luna de Madrid*, 1983).

7 Dressing up. *Manuel*.

8 Going out. *Manuel.*

9 Roberto (Jordi Mollà, left) and Carlos (Juan Diego Botto) in the bar. Montxo Armendáriz, *Historias del Kronen* (1995).

10 Carlos (left) forces Pedro (Aitor Merino) to drink at the final party. *Historias del Kronen*.

11 Juana (Pilar López de Ayala) as queen embodies the nation. Vicente Aranda, *Juana la Loca* (2001).

12 Juana as wife cares for her dying husband. *Juana la Loca*.

13 César (Eduardo Noriega) in the evacuated Gran Vía. Alejandro Amenábar, *Abre los ojos* (*Open Your Eyes*, 1997).

14 Sofia (Penélope Cruz) and César on the roof of the Picasso Tower, with the Kío Towers behind. *Abre los ojos.*

15 Marisa González, *La fábrica* (2000).

16 Marisa González, *La fábrica*.

17 Zush, *Psico-Manual-Digital* (1998).

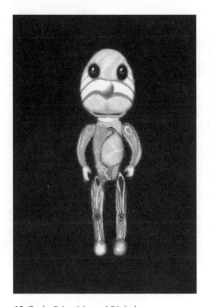

18 Zush, *Psico-Manual-Digital*.

19 Spanish women in Mexico (I): Valeria (Goya Toledo). Alejandro González Iñárritu, *Amores perros* (2000).

20 Spanish women in Mexico (II): Luisa (Maribel Verdú). Alfonso Cuarón, *Y tu mamá también* (2001).

Spanish heritage, Spanish cinema: the strange case of *Juana La Loca*

5

Between costume drama and *cine histórico*: locating nostalgia

There has been considerable focus in Spanish film studies on the relation between cinema and literature (e.g. Mínguez-Arranz 2002) and cinema and history (e.g. Talens and Zunzunegui 1995). More recently the relations between cinema, nation, and memory have been explored (Resina 2000). To my knowledge, however, no one has raised the question or indeed the possibility of a Spanish heritage cinema. This is curious because in the not dissimilar case of British film studies the topic has been much debated over a period of two decades. It might be objected that the rupture and trauma of Spanish history in the twentieth century is hardly conducive to the nostalgic pleasures of the typical British (or more properly English) period picture. Yet similarities between the two cases are clear. Post-imperial powers coping with prolonged national decline, Spain and the UK share citizens with a love of visiting heritage sites as a leisure activity. The report on cultural consumption by the SGAE (2000) notes that "visiting historical monuments," a marginal activity it defines as being "between entertainment and culture," is the most popular way for Spaniards to spend their increasing leisure time (149). Indeed, unlike most traditional activities, heritage visits are increasing year on year: in 1997, 89.7% of those interviewed admitted to some experience of this practice and 12.5% had engaged in it in the course of the past year. By 1998 the figures had risen to 93.5% and 14.0%, respectively. The SGAE laments, however, that the rich and educated have more access to such activities than the poor and unemployed. As we shall see, these demographic changes correspond with another growing leisure activity: attendance at cinemas.

Arguably, *patrimonio nacional* is more clearly and distinctly institutionalized in Spain than the UK. The most recent Academy dictionary traces the fluid link between private and public or personal and national implicit in the concept and central to heritage cinema.

Thus *patrimonio* itself is defined in family terms ("hacienda que alguien ha heredado de sus ascendientes" ["property that someone has inherited from his ancestors"]), *patrimonio nacional* in terms of a statist economy: "suma de los valores asignados ... a los recursos disponibles de un país" ("sum total of all wealth attributed ... to the disposable income of a nation") (*Diccionario* 2001). Significantly, this usage is absent from earlier editions of the dictionary. The home page of the website www.patrimonionacional.es opens confidently with a low angle, monochrome shot of the massive Royal Palace in Madrid, a transparent bid for national identity. Spanish cinema is itself clearly a further example of national heritage. Successive Royal Decrees in the 1990s were devoted to its *protección y fomento* ("protection and promotion") (*CineSpain* 2000).

In the UK, surprisingly perhaps, there seems more space for discussion, even conflict. *The New Shorter Oxford English Dictionary* (1993) defines "heritage" blandly as "that which is or may be inherited;" and gives an attributive meaning for such phrases as "heritage industry:" "concerned with the conservation and use of national or cultural heritage." The National Trust and English Heritage (equivalents of the Patrimonio Nacional) are private bodies which frequently clash with local and state governments. The former, whose role is the "preservation of places of historic interest," has faced legal battles in its attempts to declare such sites "inalienable" (National Trust 1992, 4). The Mayor of London notoriously baptized the latter the "British Taliban" for their reactionary policy towards tall buildings in the capital (Sudjic 2001).

While English has a number of terms for the genre from the academic ("heritage film") via the general ("costume drama") to the pejorative and popular ("frock flick"), the only term currently in use in Spanish film studies is *cine histórico*. This is employed simply as a marker of period and never seems to involve the problematization of history whether inside or outside of film. Moreover it represses questions of tradition and reception, property and propriety, and possession and alienation which are central to the English heritage debate and equally cogent for Spanish cinema. In *Semillas del futuro: cine español 1990–2000*, Carlos Heredero (2002) claims that *cine histórico* is itself a period piece and its presence in the 1990s a mere "inheritance" of earlier decades (76). Now Spanish cinema is "fuertemente apegado al presente" ("strongly attached to the present") (*ibid.*, 79). However he himself assembles a potential corpus of Spanish heritage movies, listing no fewer than thirty-six. Just as the lack of use of the term "heritage" or *patrimonio* in a Spanish context does not imply their irrelevance to academic debate, so the limited attention paid to *cine histórico* in Spanish surveys belies its prominence in national film production. It seems possible that this omission is related to unwelcome memories of period pictures of the Francoist period which are incompatible with the avowed modernity of contemporary Spanish cinema and its critics, strongly attached as they are to the present.

The debate becomes more urgent with the recent publication of Andrew Higson's (2003) *English Heritage, English Cinema: Costume Drama since 1980.* While Higson's own position, a stress on the political and aesthetic "ambivalence" of a genre caught between reaction and transgression, may be unchallenging, he offers an exhaustive guided tour to twenty years of film and film studies. In broad outline Higson attempts to establish a corpus and define a genre; analyse reception, especially that of film critics ambiguously related to the heritage industry; chart the industrial configuration of production, distribution, and exhibition both in the UK and US; and finally to offer two case studies: Merchant-Ivory's *Howard's End* (1992) and Shekhar Kapur's *Elizabeth* (1998). Directed, respectively, by an American and an Indian, the first film charts the menace or promise embodied by metropolitan modernity for its titular rural property, while the second follows the process through which a national icon was produced, ending as it does with the transformation of a young woman into a Virgin Queen. Both films, then, raise questions about the location of Englishness within a European and global economy; and stage the struggle for succession (of a country house, as of a country). As Higson writes:

At the centre of the narrative is a theme typical of the heritage film: not the celebration of a fixed and pure national identity, but the hesitant exploration of the crisis of inheritance, the struggle over the meaning of Englishness, and the question of national ownership. (2003, 200)

If *Elizabeth* confronts us with these "*Howard's End* questions," then, so, I would argue, does much Spanish *cine histórico*. To whom, we may ask, does Spain belong? To whom *should* it belong?

Just as Spanish period pictures have perhaps become historicized themselves (according to Heredero [2002], at least), so self-consciously innovative heritage features such as *Elizabeth* have perhaps initiated a new genre: the "post-heritage" film. Certainly Higson argues that we must follow production trends and place individual films within "cycles" (2003, 13). Looking closer at his analysis we find that it is variably relevant to the Spanish context. Thus while there is no Merchant Ivory equivalent in Spain, a prestige brand consistent in its production of literary adaptations, there is the same ambivalent tension between the literary and the historical, both laying claim to certain forms of "authenticity" (*ibid.*, 20). Generically the English heritage film draws on the intimacy of the women's picture, while concentrating on a period (1880–1940) when dominant (male) versions of national identity were being forged (*ibid.*, 25). Central to the appeal of the British genre are distinct stars, character actors, and acting styles (*ibid.*, 29) which derive from a theatrical tradition that is largely absent in Spain. Higson defends the "aesthetics of display" and "pictorialism" of film form in the genre, claiming it is by no means "uncinematic" (*ibid.*, 40). Two prominent features of mise en scène (landscape and costume) are also ambiguous. The extreme long shot of the countryside need not be fetishizing; the display of gorgeous gowns (do we look through or at them?) points either to authenticity once more or a contestation of visual display favoured by the dominant class (*ibid.*, 41). Authorship, authenticity, and irreverence are held in tension here (*ibid.*, 42). As we shall see, landscape and costume serve a similarly ambivalent function in Spanish period pictures.

British critical reception is to be seen in the context of a period in which, from Thatcher to Blair, politicians sought to rebrand an old country as "new and vibrant" (Higson 2003, 49). The collusion of film and tourism is seen most transparently in the British Tourist Authority's "movie map." But even here conflicts emerge. Foreign visitors are directed not only to the rural idylls that inspired *Howard's End* (itself, as we have seen, an ironic meditation on English inheritance) but also to the mean streets of the Edinburgh suburbs, home territory of the urban junkies of *Trainspotting*. In actorly performance, authenticity is combined with knowing pastiche, a characteristic which "enables the anomalous and perverse to be inserted into the apparently authentic historical location" (*ibid.*, 67). Past and present, fantastic and realist are blended. A similar confusion surrounds the ideological. While conservative critics celebrate the reactionary associations of a genre which prides itself on the appeal of conservation, liberal critics stress the recurrence of such themes as feminism and queer sexualities, at the very heart of English tradition (*ibid.*, 72, 73). Even nostalgia is ambivalent: "the sense of impending narrative-historical loss is ... offset by the experience of spectacular visual pleasure" (*ibid.*, 80). Period detail would thus be both the anxious response to anticipated historical trauma and the celebration of past pleasures.

Anxiety is also prominent in the commercial context. "British cinema," so-called, is a niche industry, dependent on Hollywood and TV sales, desperately seeking "crossover films" between mainstream and art house (Higson 2003, 89). Yet, we are told, by 1995 UK cinema appealed to a wider age range and more upmarket demographic (*ibid.*, 101). While the SGAE has charted similar changes for Spanish cinema audiences (especially those who favour domestic product), Spain does not benefit from the US's commercial self-interest in UK film production. As the 1990s developed, the majors launched their specialist "designer labels" (*ibid.*, 127), lending funds and taking profits from niche British titles. While they became more expert at promoting and releasing such specialized fare in the US, by the end of the decade the market was "saturated" (*ibid.*, 138) and few new UK heritage films were making an impact.

The formal properties of heritage film are also contradictory. Higson notes a troubling excess in the apparently restrained *Howard's End*. First of all there is "tension between the *narrative* critique of established national traditions and social formations and identities and the *visual* celebration of elite culture and a mythic landscape" (2003, 149). Secondly, while the narrative is slow moving and episodic and the takes long (an average of 8.92 seconds as opposed to Hollywood's 5–7 seconds) (*ibid.*, 171), shots are often "narratively unmotivated, [favouring] spectacular vantage points [which reveal] detachment from classical conventions for marking establishing and point of view shots" (*ibid.*, 172). For Higson this is the formal key to a progressive reading of the most reactionary heritage movie: "the gap between narrative requirement and the attraction of mise en scène thus allows the image to come to the fore precisely as image, as spectacle ... " (*ibid.*, 172). This troubling excess of image will recur in Spanish heritage movies.

Inversely the more overtly radical post-heritage *Elizabeth* exploits the "unrestrained" early modern period (Higson 2003, 194) to court youth and feminist audiences, those who favoured both the historical gore of *La reine Margot* (1994) and the fevered contemporaneity of *Trainspotting* (1996). Self-consciously addressing distinct "interest groups and taste communities" (*ibid.*, 196), *Elizabeth* sought to both "protect and extend" the genre (*ibid.*, 215) by posing as a hybrid "historical thriller" (211) and by employing a "relentlessly moving camera, big close ups [and] overhead shots ... a chaos of voices, music, sounds, and images" (*ibid.*, 221). In the "taste wars" (231) this "flashiness" ran the risk of falling too far downmarket and provoking a hostile reaction. The vertiginous opening sequence, which juxtaposed high angle shots of burning martyrs with decorously dancing ladies (*ibid.*, 225), was thus as violent aesthetically and generically as it was thematically. The attempt to redefine a genre is thus unstably dependent on both audience reception and authorial production, on critical response and commercial circumstance.

From national narrative to personal neurosis: Vicente Aranda's *Juana la Loca*

Elizabeth was a substantial box office hit in Spain, as throughout the world, gaining one quarter of a million admissions and making the top ten for one week. But its success cannot be compared with a local production which I take to be strictly parallel to it (and to France's *La reine Margot*), Vicente Aranda's *Juana la Loca*. It achieved some two million admissions in Spain, grossing almost 9 million euros. Opening on 28 September 2001 on 85 screens and at number seven in the box office charts (*Screen International* 2001), its only local rivals were Medem's torrid drama *Lucía y el sexo* (*Sex and Lucía*) and Santiago Segura's knowingly dumb comedy *Torrente 2*. In spite, as we shall see, of a decidedly ambivalent critical response, *Juana la Loca* clearly met a need in Spanish audiences that was not filled elsewhere. Whether we call it a heritage film or *cine histórico*, it proved to be a major cultural event in a year which *Variety*'s *International Guide* characterized as being made up of "debuts, disappointments,

and documentaries" (Cowie 2002, 306). We should begin our study
of the film by placing it within its industrial context.

As William Chislett (2002) has noted, by 2000 Spain had overtaken the US as second largest tourist destination in the world and
had no fewer than thirty-seven buildings, towns, and landscapes in
UNESCO's world heritage list. Gothic architecture was particularly
favoured (*ibid.*, 43). Official figures also show that by the late 1990s
culture and leisure had become the fourth biggest economic sector
in Spain, rising as proportion of GDP from 3.1% in 1992 to 4.46%
in 1997. Some 7.81% of employment was now in the sector, as
opposed to just 5.3% employed in the United States culture and
leisure industries (*ibid.*, 119). Film was not excluded from this
largesse: while *Variety* reported that "home grown pix gain in
Europe" and Spanish market share had grown to a high 19%
(Hopewell 2002), *Focus 2000* (European Audiovisual Observatory
2000) recorded a 17.2% increase in cinema admissions year on year
(31). Given the increasing wealth and education of Spanish audiences, conditions were ripe for a crossover film, one which (like
Elizabeth) blurred the boundaries between art house and mainstream.

Juana la Loca's budget was a relatively high 800 million pesetas;
and its twelve week shoot took place in such resonant authentic
locations as the medieval streets of Burgos (where Juana and Felipe
are proclaimed by the populace), the spectacular bridge in Toledo
(where Felipe meets Fernando el Católico to plot his wife's fate), and
the Gothic Cathedral of León (which stands in for the dramatic
courtly setting where Juana, dressed heraldically in red and yellow,
contests the attempt to certify her as insane). Other locations were
less authentic. The exteriors of the young couple's apartments were
in the Paço dos Duques de Bragança in Guimarães, Portugal. The
interiors were constructed in a Madrid studio. Confirming Higson's
judgment on the multicultural *Elizabeth* that "it is increasingly difficult to ascribe national identity to media products" (2003, 207),
Juana la Loca is also a "transnational commodity," albeit one confined to the European Union: a Hispano-Portuguese-Italian co-production. In accordance with EU regulation on such projects, high
profile roles are given to foreign participants: Felipe and Aixa-Beatriz
(the treacherous Moor) are both played by Italians dubbed into
Castilian.

Juana la Loca's authentic locations no doubt appealed to the increasing number of Spaniards who seem to find visiting historical monuments a leisure activity appropriate to moneyed, modern life. But its appeal to costume is also ambivalent, attesting both to historical authenticity (and thus the cultural prestige of the period picture) and to current fashion (and thus the more immediate visual pleasures of contemporary consumerism). Pilar López de Ayala, the young actress who won both the Goya and the *Fotogramas* award for her first starring performance, was featured in the glossies posing in medieval-style full length frocks from the current collections of such distinctive designers as veteran Sybilla and new favourite Amaya Arzuaga (Eslava Galán 2001). And when receiving her award for best actress, she favoured a model which stood out from the crowd: a floor trailing shift and overdress in contrasting green and burgundy, noticeably similar to the costumes she had worn on set. Looking both forwards and backwards (like *Elizabeth*), *Juana la Loca* attempted to appeal to both younger and older demographics. And while López de Ayala lacked the theatrical training and cachet which a British star would surely once have had (post-heritage *Elizabeth* was of course played by the Australian Cate Blanchett), she made up for it with a more useful and profitable connection, having paid her dues for several years on the teenage TV soap *Al salir de clase* (*School's Out*). In its gossipy piece on *Juana la Loca*, youth entertainment website Terra/Canal Joven (2001) detailed the travails of López de Ayala's character during the show, suggesting that the young female audience's identification and familiarity with the young star would easily cross over into the new prestige medium of feature film.

General press coverage revealed a tension over property or ownership: to whom did *Juana la Loca* belong? To whom *should* it belong? The first answer was the auteur, a 75 year old who, we are frequently told, had made twenty-four films. *El Periódico* thus claimed that *Juana la Loca* was "otra película de Vicente Aranda sobre celos y tormentos amorosos" ("another Vicente Aranda film about jealousy and the torments of love"), citing previous titles such as *La pasión turca* (*Turkish Passion*) and *Celos* (*Jealousy*) as evidence of a consistent approach to diverse material (Casas 2001). The more positive *Avui* praised the Catalan director for "una de les explosives històries d'amor que sovintegen a la seva filmografia" ("one of the explosive love stories typical of his cinematic career") (Riambau 2001). In its interview *El Semanal* also calls attention to Aranda's consistent concern for eroticism, but worries that authorial prestige is compromised by the appeal to literary mediation or precedent: Tamayo y Baus's *Locura de amor* (*Mad Love*) is a source for the script, even though it is dismissed by the director himself for its grandiloquence and by the journalist for its lack of distinction and historical accuracy (Caño Arecha 2001). Authorship, authenticity, and irreverence are here fused in unstable combination. However, there is no suggestion that the overt theatricality (even campness) of Tamayo y Baus might be read ironically as pastiche and thus productively destabilize, in post-heritage style, past and present, fantasy and history.

But for most critics the film belongs to its star. The lifestyle section of *La Vanguardia* (Rodríguez de Paz 2001) tells us López de Ayala has come "de la carpeta al corpiño" ("from satchel to corset," i.e. from school soap to period picture). *El Correo* writes (Merikaetxebarria 2001) that while there may be doubts about the film as a whole (which it calls "mediocre") there can be none about her performance in it. Even lusty young Danielle Liotti claims in *El Mundo* (Sartori 2001) to have entered acting because of a "mad love" of his own for a female celebrity whose name he cannot reveal. Just as *Elizabeth*'s critics invoked "girl power," risking anachronism and lost prestige, journalists writing on *Juana la Loca* suggest contemporary resonances whose effect on audience response to a heritage movie is difficult to predict.

Both director and actor coincide in their promotion of a "progressive" political reading of a film that is reactionary in form. Remaking or remotivating heritage, Aranda claims to be sure that "the future is female" (Caño Arecha 2001). Pilar (as the press calls her) claims repeatedly that Juana was a normal woman and that jealousy remains universal. It is an adjective also used by the director, who claims the historical setting is just "background" (Fotograma.com 2001). In the "making of" documentary included on the DVD, Aranda claims that Felipe's promiscuity was just part of his political "liberalism," echoing the words put into the mouth of the Flemish courtier de Veyre. Felipe was, it appears, a proto-bourgeois in a reactionary, fanatical Spain. The debate around the conservative or liberal implications of the heritage movie is thus both acted out in *Juana la Loca*'s critical reception and projected back into the film itself, where it becomes an implausible, even anachronistic, topic of discussion.

The problem of the period intersects with that of national territory. Aranda claims bullishly (Fotograma.com 2001) that had Juana la Loca lived outside Spain she would be considered an "exceptional figure". Moreover he is aware that the film will not be understood in the same way from one country to another. Failing to appear at the Goya awards, where Amenábar's *The Others* was the great winner (and raised hackles as to the authenticity of its "Spanishness"), Aranda complained that a genre film on the "living dead" should not be in competition with his own historical picture. Yet he is aware that the heritage movie is not universally praised, claiming defensively that *Juana la Loca*'s critical and commercial success "ha acabado con la discriminación de los cineastas veteranos y con la que sufre el cine histórico" ("ended the discrimination against veteran filmmakers and period films"). Indeed when the film received a limited US release critics were hardly respectful: the *New York Times* wrote of "a historical spectacle made for late-night cable viewing" (Mitchell 2002); the *San Francisco Examiner* praised repeatedly (and ironically) the "fabulous period costumes" (Anderson 2002); the *Village Voice* called it a "Hallmark special" (Atkinson 2002). While British heritage films could rely on the familiarity of Masterpiece Theatre to presell costume drama to select US audiences familiar with and friendly towards English actors, themes, and locations, *Juana la Loca*, stripped of national context and lacking in US commercial connections, failed to achieve distinction abroad.

How, then, do we read the formal properties of the film? While the palette is relatively sober (with many of the costumes restricted to burgundy and dark green) and the shooting style plain, the mise en scène does tend towards those ambivalent moments of excess to which Higson (2003) calls attention. The opening shot of Tordesillas, where the aged Juana is confined, is from a showy low angle, with black clouds speeding ominously across the sky above. It is a camera position that is repeated in front of imposing facades throughout the film. Cutting to a dark interior where Juana faces the fire, Aranda dissolves from the portrait of Felipe in 1554 to the same picture in 1496, when the young Juana is being taken to meet her future husband. In the credit sequence which follows, the camera stands placidly for a lengthy 65 seconds as the retinue parades on horses before us. Later Isabel la Católica's remaining children are posed stiffly before us while the male narrator intones their names. Aranda could hardly signal more clearly his bid for cultural capital: the deceleration of Hollywood cutting and camera movement is agonizingly evident. Yet even here the quest for authority is undermined. It took a German critic to note that the pompous tones of the narrator are indistinguishable from those of Francoist newsreel (*Filmzeitschrift* 2003).

Long takes and limited camera movement are complemented by camera distance. Rejecting closeups, except in his trademark irreverent sex scenes, Aranda keeps the camera in long shot even in the climactic sequence, which comes some thirty leisurely minutes in, when Juana betrays the first signs of madness, screaming of her mother's death and her husband's infidelity as rain drenches her in the palace patio. Extreme closeups are reserved for two key contrasting props: the golden top given to Juana by her childhood lover and the magic charm used by Felipe's Moorish lover to ensnare him. Aranda also cuts for contrast: the black clad funeral of Juana's brother leads into the birth of her first daughter; the daylight exterior where the new monarchs are displayed to cheering crowds is contrasted with the nocturnal interior where Felipe first encounters the fatal belly dancer. While this alternation lends some narrative pace to a slow moving episodic script, it falls far short of the shocking extravagance and violence of *Elizabeth*'s crosscutting.

Juana's transformation scene, in which she appears to her nobles for the first time in the guise of a ruling monarch, which is once more parallel to that of *Elizabeth*, also falls flat. Only seconds after subduing her rebellious court as the embodiment of Castile (castles and lions are appliquéd on her robes) and abusing her philandering husband as a "puppet" of his court (Figure 11), she has changed into less sumptuous costume and is tearfully embracing Felipe's wounds (Figure 12). The ideological ambiguity of the heritage picture (conservative or liberal, progressive or reactionary?), addressed explicitly in the film's production and reception, here registers not as suggestive ambivalence but as pure incoherence, transgressing the minimal grounds of psychological plausibility. Proto-feminism and royalist nostalgia prove irreconcilable.

Higson's (2003) most valuable suggestion is that there is a tension between narrative and spectacle in the heritage film: while the

first is often progressive, stressing the conflicts at the heart of inheritance, the second is generally reactionary, consoling threatened
audiences for the loss of imperial power or class privilege. As a historical and narrative character Juana la Loca could hardly be more
apt an embodiment of the trouble in heritage. Indeed the whole film
is devoted to the question: "To whom should Spain (or Castile)
belong?". This national or historical narrative cannot, however, be
integrated into the personal drama which Aranda and López de
Ayala claim is universal and, indeed, contemporary. And it is muted
by an unexceptional visual regime which fails to offer that fragile
and troubling excess which might call into question a national identity rather than flattering and consoling it for the wounds of history.
Aranda's mythic landscape of arid mesetas and bleak castles may be
less lush than the green meadows and country houses of Merchant
Ivory; it is no less mediocre in its vision of Spanish heritage and its
contribution to Spanish cinema.

However, the interest of Aranda's film lies precisely in its incoherence, in the transparency with which it crystallizes cultural contradictions widespread in the Spain of the 1990s. Some critics
complained that *Juana la Loca* reduced national history to personal
neurosis (e.g. Martín 2001). But if we were to reread this neurosis
as belonging to the film rather than to its main character, we might
begin an alternative diagnosis. After all, neurosis is defined psycho-
analytically as an "affection in which the symptoms are the symbolic expression of a psychical conflict whose origins lie in the
subject's childhood history" (Laplanche and Pontalis 1998, s.v.
"neurosis"). Paralysed, like the neurotic, "between desire and
defence," *Juana la Loca* can be read as an example of *cine histórico*
which is truly, technically neurotic, beyond the reassuring boundaries of Higson's heritage movie.

Works cited

Caño Arecha, Juan. 'Vicente Aranda: "Estoy seguro de que el
    futuro es de las mujeres."' [interview] *El Semanal: Encuentros*
    30 September 2001, 17–19.
Casas, Quim. '*Juana la Loca*, otra película de Vicente Aranda sobre
    celos y tormentos amorosos.' [review] *El Periódico: Agenda*
    30 September 2001, 2.

Chislett, William. *The Internationalization of the Spanish Economy*. Madrid: Elcano, 2002.

Cowie, Peter (ed.). *Variety International Film Guide 2003*. London: Button, 2002.

Diccionario de la Lengua Española. Madrid: Real Academia Española, 2001.

Eslava Galán, Juan. 'Juana no estaba tan loca.' *El Mundo: Magazine* 23 September 2001, 20–3.

European Audiovisual Observatory. *Focus 2000: World Film Market Trends*. Cannes, 2000.

Heredero, Carlos. *Semillas de futuro: cine español 1990–2001*. Madrid: Nuevo Milenio, 2002.

Higson, Andrew. *English Heritage, English Cinema: Costume Drama Since 1980*. Oxford: Oxford University Press, 2003.

Hopewell, John. 'Homegrown pix gain ground at Euro B.O.: Spain.' *Variety* 24 December 2001–6 January 2002, 13.

Laplanche, J. and Pontalis, J. B. *The Language of Psychoanalysis*. London: Karnak, 1988.

Martín, Jerónimo J. '¿Juana la Loca o Juana la Obsesa?' *La Gaceta: Fin de Semana* 29 September 2001, 7.

Merikaetxebarria, Antón. 'Un amor de perdición.' [review] *El Correo* 26 September 2001, 83.

Mínguez-Arranz, Norberto (ed.). *Literatura española y cine*. Madrid: Complutense, 2002.

National Trust. *The National Trust Handbook*. London, 1992.

New Shorter Oxford English Dictionary. Oxford: Oxford University Press, 1993.

Resina, Joan Ramon. 'Short of memory: the reclamation of the past since the Spanish transition to democracy.' In Resina (ed.), *Disremembering the Dictatorship*. Amsterdam: Rodopi, 2000, 83–125.

Riambau, Esteve. 'Amour fou.' [review] *Avui: Espectacles* 29 September 2001, 50.

Rodríguez de Paz, Alicia. 'De la carpeta al corpiño.' [actor profile] *La Vanguardia: Vivir* 24 September 2001, 9.

Screen International. 'International Box Office.' 5 October 2001, 26.

SGAE. *Hábitos de consumo cultural*. Madrid: SGAE, 2000.

Talens, Jenaro, and Zunzuzegui, Santos. *Rethinking Film History: History as Narration*. Valencia: Episteme, 1995.

Electronic sources

Anderson, Jeffrey M. Review of *Juana la Loca*. *San Francisco Examiner*
6 September 2002. Accessed 18 April 2003.
www.examiner.com/movies/default.jsp?story=
X0906MADLOVEw
Atkinson, Michael. Review of *Juana la Loca*. *Village Voice*
28 August–3 September 2002. Accessed 18 April 2003.
www.villagevoice.com/issues/0235/atkinson.php
CineSpain. 'Legislación.' 9 June 2000. www.cinespain.com/
ICAA/cifras/index.php
Filmzeitschrift. Review of *Juana la Loca*. Accessed 18 April 2003.
www.filmzeitschrift.de/berlinale/special/sebastian/html
Fotograma.com. 'España va al Oscar con *Juana la Loca*.'
12 November 2001. Accessed 18 April 2003.
www.fotograma.com/ notas/actualidad/1919.shtml
Mitchell, Elvis. Review of *Juana la Loca*. *New York Times* 30 August
2002. Accessed 18 April 2003.
www.nytimes.com/ 2002/08/30/movies/30MAD.html
Patrimonio Nacional. Accessed 18 April 2003.
www.patrimonionacional.com
Sartori, Beatriz. 'Danielle Liotti.' *Elmundo.es* 28 September 2001.
Accessed 18 April 2003.
www.el-mundo.es/laluna/2001/ 142/1001510919.html
Sudjic, Dejan. 'A Thoroughly Modernizing Mayor.' *Observer*
[London] 8 July 2001. Accessed 28 September 2003.
http:// observer.guardian.co.uk/print/0,3858,4217791-
102280,00. html
Terra/Canal Joven. 'Descúbrelo ... Pilar López de Ayala.'
13 November 2001. Accessed 18 April 2003.
www.terra.es/ joven/articulo/html/jov5667.htm

6

High anxiety: Amenábar's *Abre los ojos* (*Open Your Eyes*)/ Crowe and Cruise's *Vanilla Sky*

Between Europe and the US: locating remakes

As several critics have noted, remakes produce anxiety. In their introduction to a collective volume on the theme Andrew Horton and Stuart Y. McDougal (1998) inadvertently suggest a source of this concern. They write: "We are concerned with remakes as aesthetic or cinematic texts and as ideological expressions of cultural discourse set in particular times, contexts, and societies" (*ibid.*, 1) This conflict between the formal and the industrial, arguably inherent in the whole of cinema, is staged with particular intensity in the remake. Lucy Mazdon (2000) maps the binary of quality (high/low) onto nationality (Europe/US), citing a British critic for whom "fine Continental fare" is transformed into the "sensationalist pap" of Hollywood (1). But this cultural distinction is by no means inherent to the films themselves. Rather it is a function of the remake process: however vacuous the French originals may be, critics tend to lend status to the source films (and conversely deprive the US remakes of the same) simply because of their national origin (*ibid.*, 2). While the critical work on such films is "overwhelmingly negative" it is, for Mazdon, problematic to attribute value: French "originals" are by no means necessarily better than American "copies" (*ibid.*, 5). Although it is correct to decry the asymmetry of distribution by which European films are denied access to US theatres, "it is not French 'art' which is 'under threat' from the remake but rather those popular domestic genres [such as comedy] often despised by the critics" (*ibid.*, 92). Close empirical studies such as Mazdon's thus undermine the aesthetic and ideological biases against remakes.

More recently Jennifer Forrest and Leonard R. Koos have gone further in "reviewing remakes" (2002, 1), tracing a history of the denunciation of "cultural piracy and political imperialism" (*ibid.*, 5) which has remained unchanged for forty years. Thus for Ginette Vincendeau in 1992 the "uniqueness of French 'family narrative'" ("deeply rooted in cultural difference") is "untranslatable," containing elements which US remakes "brazenly [and mistakenly] assume to be universal" (*ibid.*, 7). The only exception to this is the rare case of an "original" that is "already Americanized." Such prejudices go back to Bazin in 1952, when, already, "European films ... assume[d] a noncommercial aura" (*ibid.*, 12). The binaries underwriting this critical discourse are clear: US commercialism favours clear cut motivation in both causality and character, where plots arrive at a comforting resolution; French artistry tends towards ambiguity and disconcertingly open endings (*ibid.*, 8). Now, as then, such distinctions are problematic. As Forrest and Koos write, Hollywood has always been an "international cinematic community" (*ibid.*, 9). Moreover the "audience helping to mold the form that [US] ideology takes is decidedly international" (*ibid.*, 16). The supposedly inherent distinction that maps high and low onto French and American cinema is thus empirically incorrect (the great majority of French cinema, including those films chosen for remakes, is commercial by nature). But it is also industrial not aesthetic in origin, a function of particular distribution practices and market segmentation:

Historically industries that have been squeezed out of competition in one sector of the market normally react with a reconceptualization of their market, as in a shift from mass production to that of quality. (Forrest and Koos 2002, 16)

Bazin's hostility to the remake thus betrays a broader ideological bias: "[he] cannot reconcile the economics of film production with the romantic notion of the inviolability of the original" (*ibid.*, 20).

It is instructive to shift our gaze for a moment from academic criticism to the trade press. A survey in *Screen International* asks "What makes a good remake?" (Frater and Kay 2003). Interestingly the authors repeat the gastronomic metaphors used by film critics: "Hollywood's voracious appetite for material can often mean a cannibalization of itself and a hunger for exotic fare" (*ibid.*, 9). One Asian producer notes that "Hollywood got bored of European films and has imported Asian horror and Hong Kong action" (*ibid.*). This shift in remake focus is said to be based on the nature of the films themselves, boasting as they do "good structure and surprises" and "more high concept than European films:" "You need a strong concept, strong characters, several good scenes that you can build a movie around" (*ibid.*). Most such Asian originals belong to three genres: "action-thriller, horror, or comedy." These are films which are easier to sell because they exhibit clearer "trailer moments" than, say, dramas. Elsewhere *Screen International* reminds us that "the remake game is not a one-way process: a growing number of US and international films are being reworked for local audiences" (Shackleton, Rodier and Zagt 2003, 11). It follows, then, that in contemporary cinema remakes cannot be reduced to the binaries of high/low or European/American. The unambiguous pleasures of the well defined narrative ("high concept," "trailer moment") are now as native to Japan and Hong Kong as they are to the US. To stigmatize such films as "already Americanised" would be misguided.

If Asian cinema is a third term disrupting familiar oppositions between European art and American commerce, then distinctions remain within Europe itself. Very few Hollywood remakes have been of Spanish films and what literature remains is inadequate. When Lucy Fischer (1998), a specialist in Hollywood melodrama, wrote on Almodóvar's *Tacones lejanos* (*High Heels*) (a partial remake of Sirk's *Imitation of Life*) she was so insensitive to Spanish context as to misspell the names of characters and, indeed, of the director. And she argues, mistakenly, that "*High Heels* circulates in elitist film markets" (*ibid.*, 202). While the limited distribution of foreign language film makes this true of the US, it can hardly be the case in Spain or, indeed, France, where Almodóvar's films are massively popular at the box office (Lumiere). Before treating a rare and valuable example of a Spanish film remade by Hollywood – Alejandro Amenábar's *Abre los ojos* (*Open Your Eyes*) (1997) – it is necessary, then, to make a detour through the Spanish context of production, distribution, and exhibition, which is generally neglected by critics and yet is inseparable from the questions of cultural value and circulation we have seen in the remake debate.

In the 1990s Spanish cinema became a most unlikely but welcome success story. Feature production rose from a low of 44 in 1994 to a high of 82 in 1999; and by the end of the decade Spanish film achieved wider international distribution than countries with better-known cinematic traditions such as Italy and Germany (Ministerio de Cultura). Commercial success was matched by artistic ambition: Spanish films regularly won prizes at festivals; and filmmakers during the decade include a startling number of first time directors, including several women (Heredero 1997, 28). Spanish films remained idiosyncratic, but now combining traditional strengths in characterization and shooting with new found skills in plotting and editing, they learned to reconcile local traditions with the Hollywood model and thus attract younger and wider audiences. Technical facilities in postproduction were also much improved, enabling a "quality look" previously lacking. The official report on *World Film Market Trends* by the European Audiovisual Observatory showed a "massive 17.1% growth" in cinema audiences in 1999, "almost compensating on its own," it writes, "for falls on the other European markets" (European Audiovisual Observatory 2000, 5). Average admissions in Spain rose to twice those in Italy and Germany. Moreover Spanish share in the domestic market rose to a healthy 13.8% (*ibid.*, 31).

The central paradox of Spanish cinema of the 1990s is precisely this persistence of quality and quantity in a time of reduced domestic subsidies and cutthroat competition in an increasingly global market. I have two hypotheses for explaining this miraculous survival. The first is the persistence of locality in an international culture. There is evidence, both statistical and anecdotal, that Spanish audiences increasingly do not always welcome US pictures and are not the passive dupes of Hollywood they might be thought. A trivial point: the difficulty for Spanish customers in pronouncing the title *Eyes Wide Shut*, which remained untranslated (Naumann 1999); the same film prompted one viewer, albeit a reader of conservative daily *ABC*, to protest at gratuitous sex scenes and praise the "quality" of Spanish cinema (Pérez Templado 1999). In spite of isolated cases of hugely popular coarse comedies, there was a certain drift up-market, which can also be seen in the case of Spanish television where domestically produced quality series drama began to draw higher ratings than American product (Smith 2003, 22).

This rise in quality corresponded to changes in audience demographic. Far from dumbing down, as stereotype suggests, Spanish audiences for both film and TV have been trickling up. Recent research has shown that cinema audiences in Spain are now wealthier and better educated than before. While they remain relatively young (Spanish audiences tail off after age 45), they are now overwhelmingly metropolitan and benefit from higher education. Moreover domestic product is favoured by such choice demographic segments as women and graduates (SGAE 2000, 148–9). The Spanish quality TV phenomenon, led by private webs such as Tele 5, is thus related to the commercial success of artistically demanding features such as Almodóvar's recent releases. If locality pays, then quality makes money for a new more educated audience.

Considerable attention has been paid to film production in 1990s Spain, including the exemplary studies of Carlos F. Heredero (1997, 1999). Domestic journalists have lamented the more recent reduction in the number of features made and deplore government and TV finance for the film industry that makes Spain the worst funded of the big five European nations. Paradoxically, however, regular positive features on Spain have appeared in English language trade magazines such as *Variety*: typical headlines read "Int'l success at last: sales push Spanish helmers beyond auteur status;" and "The gain in Spain ... falls mainly on a recent burst of hit local pix" (Hopewell, April and August 1999). US product has thus not benefited as greatly as expected from the multinationals' multiplexing of Spain, a process that has occurred later than in other European territories and has led to increased admissions. The secret of Spanish cinema's success, more visible perhaps to anxious American exporters than to pessimistic local commentators, may thus lie more in distribution and exhibition than in production: the skillful marketing and the more comfortable screening of features that are more in tune than they once were with a changing public.

I would now like to examine the filmmaker I believe to be most representative of the trends in contemporary Spanish cinema I sketched out above: Alejandro Amenábar. Amenábar's brief history is well known. Born to a Chilean father and Spanish mother in Santiago in 1972 and taken to Spain as a child just before the fall of Allende, Amenábar attended the film school at Madrid's Complutense University, where he famously failed to complete the course (Heredero 1997, 89). Later voluble in interviews on the irrelevance and incompetence of his training (citing an assignment on "Defamiliarization in *The Guns of Navarone*" as evidence), his revenge at the age of just twenty-four was *Tesis* (*Thesis*) (1996), a sleek, taut thriller on the theme of snuff movies in which the serial killer, a professor of media studies, was given the same name as one of Amenábar's unlucky teachers. After winning no fewer than eight Goya awards, including best picture, *Tesis* proved a sensational debut, gaining almost one million admissions in Spain (Ministerio de Cultura) and attracting overwhelmingly positive press.

A recent book on Amenábar rehearses the main features of his short career: his contempt for an artificial or "orthopaedic" cinema; his "curious recycling" of earlier films and genres; the power of the public over his vision; the difficult balance between US and European influences; the closeness of his youthful characters to his audience; the solidity of his narrative structure and stylistic resources; and finally his unashamed editorializing on issues such as media violence and urban alienation (Sempere 2000, 35–45).

More importantly, perhaps, Amenábar's position in the field of Spanish cinema corresponds to the criteria I sketched earlier, thus making him the most representative of recent directors. Typical of the 1990s renaissance, he was a first time director who combined from the start of his career commercial success with artistic ambition, pleasing both public and critics. Technically gifted, he lends his images a quality look which rivals Hollywood, backed up by relatively high budgets secured by a veteran producer, José Luis Cuerda. Visually brilliant, his films are also surprisingly literate, incorporating ironic commentaries on themselves into their complex narratives. And featuring some unexpected shifts in gender positions, they also please the newly up-market demographic: educated, urban, and possibly female. Moreover Amenábar's ambitions move before production into promotion and distribution. *Abre los ojos* benefited, unusually for a Spanish film of the period, from an ambitious website featuring, in addition to two trailers, a graphic giving access to the various locations of the film, all set to the ominous theme composed by Amenábar himself. And with its high concept and glossy style *Abre los ojos* could hold its own against US competition in the new city multiplexes that are the preferred sites for Spanish exhibitors. Amenábar's third feature, *The Others* (a critically praised English-language horror movie starring Nicole Kidman), reconfirmed his ability to marry art and commerce.

Where Spanish critics had attacked Almodóvar in the 1980s for daring to invoke Hollywood figures such as Sirk as inspiration, curiously they supported Amenábar in his somewhat similar admiration for Hitchcock. I would suggest that this critical consensus (marred only by some criticism of Amenábar's narrative skills) marked what Bourdieu has called the "circle of consecration" (1996, 482). Novel but not unprecedented, Spanish but not parochial, challenging but not overly demanding of their audience, Amenábar's features satisfied both the subjective dispositions of their director and the objective conditions newly required of Spanish cinema. Marketed as part of a new generation of filmmakers, Amenábar openly proclaimed the industrial context which produced and welcomed him: the professor-cum-serial killer of *Tesis* famously makes a speech claiming that Spanish cinema must please the audience if it is successfully to compete with Hollywood.

From *casticismo* to cosmopolitanism: *Abre los ojos* and *Vanilla Sky*

Abre los ojos, Amenábar's second feature, internalizes the two factors that I proposed earlier as most characteristic of recent Spanish cinema: innovation within genre frameworks and localization of culture. But first a plot synopsis:

Abre los ojos (*Open Your Eyes*) (Spain-France-Italy 1997)
A prison cell in an unnamed city, the present. César (Eduardo Noriega), a twenty-five year old in a prosthetic mask, tells his story to a psychiatrist. Rich and good looking, César was attractive to women. At his birthday party he flirts successfully with beautiful Sofía (Penélope Cruz), the girlfriend of his best friend, Pelayo (Fele Martínez). The next morning he accepts a lift from his obsessive ex-lover, Nuria (Nawja Nimri). She crashes the car, committing suicide, and César is horribly disfigured, beyond the help of cosmetic surgery. No longer handsome, he discovers Sofía is now more comfortable with Pelayo. In a drunken stupor César falls asleep in the street. On awakening everything has changed: Sofía now claims to love him and the surgeons restore his lost looks. But making love to Sofía one night, she apparently changes into Nuria. Horrified, César murders her, yet finds that everyone else believes that Nuria was indeed Sofía.

While he is confined to the prison, fragments of his past return to him as if in a dream. César becomes aware that he had visited a company called Life Extension. Returning to their headquarters, under strict supervision, he discovers that they specialize in cryogenics with a twist: "artificial perception" or the provision of a fantasy based on his past life to a client who is reborn in the future. Convinced that his life since the drunken night in the street is simply a nightmarish vision created by Life Extension, César leaps from the roof of the company's high rise headquarters, resolving to open his eyes once more to real life outside the cryogenic fantasy.

In its narrative *Abre los ojos* clearly exemplifies Amenábar's two editorial issues: urban alienation and the danger of the image. Vitality has been replaced by virtuality, life by life extension. If we examine two sequences, however, we will see how the related themes of dislocation of the city and defacement of the self relate to film form as well as content.

In the credit sequence the emblematically named César awakes in his studiously anonymous apartment (all glass brick and stripped wood) to discover as he drives through the streets that the city has been evacuated: he is left roaming a deserted boulevard, skyscrapers in the distance. Typically assured and disorientating, the sequence begins with extreme closeups and proceeds through travelling and point of view shots to end with a rare crane shot, magnifying the void at the heart of the city and diminishing the lone figure on the street (Figure 13). The sequence, now revealed as a dream, begins once more, this time with César disposing dismissively of his girlfriend Nuria and cruising the city streets, now choked as normal with traffic and pedestrians, including homeless people and a film crew.

Spanish critics such as Sempere have generally proclaimed the cosmopolitanism of Amenábar (2000, 40), implying that *Tesis* or *Abre los ojos* could have been shot in Paris or New York as easily as in Madrid. While it is true that Amenábar makes no explicit reference in either film to the city in which the action takes place, it remains the case, however, that the alienation effect (the sudden sense of foreignness) can only be fully experienced by those who recognize the film's loaded location: Madrid's Gran Vía (the equivalent of Broadway or Shaftesbury Avenue); and, even more emblematically, the Plaza de España, in which Penélope Cruz is briefly glimpsed as a white faced mime. Indeed Amenábar has spoken in interview of the difficulty of emptying this most chaotic and traffic choked highway for the shoot and of his familiarity with the homeless people whom he sought, briefly, to immortalize. Moreover the contrast between the eerily evacuated city and the conventionally crowded urban landscape would be considerably less in other modern metropolises, such as many in the US and UK, which do not share the density of population and richness of street life of the Spanish capital. *Abre los ojos*' urban alienation, then, supposedly cosmopolitan, relies on local knowledge of its setting to achieve full effect. Indeed the mise en scène is strikingly reminiscent of a celebrated graphic precedent: Antonio López's monumental paintings of an equally eery depopulated Gran Vía.

In a second sequence dislocation is combined with defacement. César, supposedly cured of his disfigurement, rises from bed once more only to discover he is terribly disfigured once again. As in the credit sequence, this is a dream. The sequence repeats and he returns relieved to bed. This time however it is Sofía who has changed, with saintly Penélope Cruz replaced by unsettling Nawja Nimri. Using extreme closeups and point of view shots once more, Amenábar has the spectator participate in his protagonist's disorientation, thus creating narrative suspense.

Moreover focusing as the film does on male narcissism (and thus inverting the traditional gender binaries), *Abre los ojos* renders the female object disturbingly mutable, replaceable, and prone to loss. It is this insistence on a double loss and a double obsession that marks Amenábar's closest allegiance to the Hitchcock of *Vertigo*. But it also marks a defamiliarization of the male body, newly eroticized in the figure of youthful Eduardo Noriega and as prone as the female to fragility, degradation, and loss. The traditional Spanish male is thus doubly lost: alienated from a city that is emptied of its dense sociality; distanced from a self that can no longer rely on a female to prop up its fragile sense of self. The two themes of dislocation and defacement, ably enacted through shooting and editing, are thus mutually reinforcing.

If city and self are no longer recognizable, then the same is true of Spanish cinema: Amenábar's thrillers lack the *costumbrismo* and *casticismo* (attention to Spanish customs and "purity" of tradition) of an earlier era. But just as their novelty is only relative (indeed, is openly dependent on prestigious precedents), so their cosmopolitanism in only skin deep: the thrill of the *Unheimlich* relies, as ever, on familiarity with the *Heim* that is so slightly subverted. The motif of repetition so prominent in both clips, however, is more than the "slavish postmodernism" so loosely invoked in Spain (Smith 2000, 69). Rather it suggests that relative innovation demanded of an audiovisual market that must combine novelty with accessibility, imagination with profit. If the 1990s renaissance of Spanish film, so widely celebrated, seemed threatened in the following decade (and the recent statistics suggest that this is the case), then Amenábar's ambiguous thrillers, at once domestic and international, novel and traditional, remain one of the most important examples of a film practice that combines art and commerce. Indeed they serve as a plausible model outside Spain for a European cinema that bridges the gap between art house and mainstream.

Returning to remakes, then, it seems no accident that *Abre los ojos*, apparently "already Americanized," should have been one of the very few Spanish features to be remade in Hollywood. Cameron Crowe's *Vanilla Sky* (2001), starring and co-produced by Tom Cruise, is unnervingly close to its original. The IMDb gives no fewer than eleven keywords that coincide: asylum (or "mental institution"), cryogenics, mask, murder, psychiatrist, suicide, car accident, disfigurement, dream, jealousy, nightmare, surreal. Moreover the innovative fusion of genres remains the same, given by the website for both films as: drama, romance, sci-fi, and thriller. Details frequently recur in identical form, not just in the dialogue but also in setting, cinematography, and even lighting: Life Extension keeps its original (English) name; the doctors sit at a semicircular table (required in the original because of a unique location, the round viewing room atop the Madrid tower known as El Faro de la Moncloa); when César imagines Sofía and his best friend meeting behind his back, Crowe, like Amenábar, breaks briefly into black and white; the nightclub scene is lit in both films by blue lasers that weave a web over the actors' heads.

But where Amenábar's Madrid is relatively dislocated (the Gran Vía goes apparently unrecognized by Spanish critics, El Faro de la Moncloa is relatively unknown), Crowe and Cruise are insistent on the New York location of *Vanilla Sky*. The very first shots are dreamy aerial views of instantly recognizable midtown skyscrapers and Central Park, floating down to the Dakota Building where media magnate David (Cruise) lives in conspicuous luxury. (Conversely César's loft could be anywhere.) Penelope Cruz, repeating her performance in *Abre los ojos* and retaining the name of Sofía, lives in the shadow of the Manhattan Bridge. And if US audiences fail to recognize the exact location, they must surely be familiar with the "uptown"/"downtown" distinction which maps the opposition between wealthy privilege and impoverished chic so clearly onto city geography. Specific New York motifs recur throughout the film, from the Macy's Parade (giant inflatables visible from David's apartment window) to Conan O'Brien on the late show. There are no equivalents in *Abre los ojos*, which studiously avoids such specific cultural markers. And where César merely mentions the business associates who control the catering company he inherited, David is shown repeatedly confronting the elderly board of his publishing empire at meetings and parties. Confirming a familiar cliché, *Vanilla Sky* shows us that the business of New York is indeed business.

Some twenty minutes longer than the original, *Vanilla Sky* is conspicuously overemphatic, both formally and conceptually. While Amenábar's dialogue is terse and his actors' performance style underplayed, Crowe opts for repeated and anxious underlining. Brian (David's sidekick, Amenábar's Pelayo) says of Sofía: "She could be, could be, could be, the fucking girl of my dreams." Cruise's winning smile is greatly overused in the first half hour. The Madrid Sofía favours loose fitting but unexceptional sweaters; the New York Sofía attends a swish uptown party in a huge anorak, which is repeatedly commented on in the dialogue. The role of the Spanish language is also important here. In *Abre los ojos* Cruz is just another local girl, albeit unusually winsome and lovely. In *Vanilla Sky* she is above all foreign, given a surname that will evoke fancy gastronomy to English speakers (Serrano, from *jamón serrano*, cured ham) and prone to outbursts in rapid fire Spanish which David finds charmingly unintelligible. (Cruise himself, a better businessman than his character, takes care to greet the Spanish press in correct Castilian.)

In his commentary to the US DVD, Cameron Crowe generously acknowledges his debt to Amenábar, citing such "homages" as the opening shot in *Vanilla Sky* when the words "Open your eyes" are recited over a black screen in the original Spanish. The anxiety inherent in the remake as a genre is here rendered more acute by the unusual closeness of the two films, a closeness which tends to switch stereotypes of the European and American. It is the economical Amenábar who strips away all superfluous elements in the service of a smoothly functioning plot: *Abre los ojos* is truly high concept. For all its overemphasis, *Vanilla Sky* remains highly ambiguous. Indeed the director's commentary revels in this ambiguity, suggesting there are at least four mutually exclusive readings of the plot. Crowe claims in contradictory fashion: "It isn't obvious, it's a movie to watch closely … [and] it's a movie to let wash over you."

This sensory and conceptual overloading is so dense and continuous as to be subliminal, requiring the perfect freeze frame of the DVD to be properly explored. Thus as David awakes in his huge uptown apartment *Sabrina* is playing on his flat screen TV (specially designed by Cruise for the film). This is the first of a series of references to Audrey Hepburn that Crowe claims run through the film. These references tend to work against *Vanilla Sky*'s narrative and visual impact: Cruz's unflattering costume in the final sequence (a brown woolen suit) is apparently another Hepburn reference, but is far less effective cinematically than the flimsy white gown she had worn in the original climax high on the roof of a Madrid skyscraper (Figure 14). The flashing screens of Times Square momentarily show Jann Wenner, the founder of *Rolling Stone*, whom Crowe claims as a precedent for Cruise's character. The cacophonous soundtrack, often willfully incongruous (the Beach Boys' "Good Vibrations" plays over David's final torment) could not be further from Amenábar's self-penned score, modestly tailored to reinforce each plot point. Even the most hostile of European critics could not claim in this case that Hollywood had sacrificed formal complexity to clarity of exposition and reassuring resolution.

Let us examine, briefly, the equivalents of the two scenes I discussed earlier in *Abre los ojos*. While the opening dream of the evacuated city is shown by Amenábar in just over a minute and only nineteen different shots, Crowe precedes it with the aerial views of Manhattan (thus confusingly locating a dream in a very precise geography) and extends it over nearly four minutes and innumerable quick cuts. As mentioned already, the opening interior is more cluttered than Amenábar's, with *Sabrina* already showing on David's TV. Crowe's equivalent of the Gran Vía is Times Square, perhaps the only place to function in the same way in the US as the original location does in Spain. It is typical of *Vanilla Sky*'s emphasis (or overemphasis) on location that in a production that lists over one hundred credits for digital and visual effects, the publicity stressed that Times Square really was shut down for this opening sequence. But where César is shown in a single long shot disappearing silently into the empty avenue, David runs at speed through the street, cross-cut with near subliminal advertising images and set to the habitual cacophonous soundtrack. Crowe thus sacrifices the formal and thematic point of the sequence (the individual's fear of isolation within the city) to an excess of visual and auditory stimulation that remains difficult to interpret. This is not to say that the Spanish "original" is superior to the US "copy," but rather that the European version is more "Hollywood" than the American, more focused on and directed towards narrative and psychological coherence.

The two versions of the "defacement" scene in which the women are exchanged are rather similar. Amenábar said in the UK press book (Redbus 1999, unpaginated) that his priority in this film was camera placement and point of view: the problem was how to suggest to the audience that some sequences are to be read as the protagonist's fantasy. In Crowe's version Cruise's performance is typically overemphatic: unlike the more controlled Noriega, he pulls a grotesque face at himself in the mirror even after he has been reassured that he has not lost his good looks once again. But where Amenábar shows the substitution of Sofía by Nawja Nimri's Nuria strictly from César's perspective (his fingers fondle a lock of too short hair beneath the sheets), Crowe shoots objectively, having Cameron Diaz's Julie reappear from under the bedclothes while David is also in shot. The narrative tension and suspense of classic Hollywood plotting and shooting is thus lost and the consistency of point of view confused.

Vanilla Sky received a mixed critical reception (*Rotten Tomatoes*) but its box office benefited from a world promotional tour by its stars (a documentary is included as an extra on the US DVD). Proving the exclusion of foreign language films from US distribution, *Abre los ojos* had been seen by only 72,976 Americans. Conversely *Vanilla Sky* had grossed over $100 million in the US and had been seen by half a million people in Spain (IMDb). In spite of the media blitz, however, the numbers reconfirmed the relative independence of

Spanish audiences, who do not always succumb to the seductions of Hollywood. Amenábar's original had been seen by 1,794,037 Spaniards, more than three times the audience of Crowe's (Ministerio de Cultura). Unsurprisingly the Madrid premiere was conflictive. *El País* reported that Cruise and Cruz stopped the traffic on the "old Gran Vía" (Fernández-Santos 2002), ironically just as Amenábar had during the shoot five years earlier. Although the Spanish press congratulated Cruise on his Spanish, they made "continuous comparisons" with Amenábar's version, obliging the stars to deny the new film was just a "copy." This question of authenticity extended to the couple's private life, with newspapermen demanding to know if their rumoured love affair was a publicity stunt.

What we have seen, however, is that the loaded distinction between "original" and "copy" is inadequate to account for the artistic and industrial qualities of remakes, especially when it is unthinkingly mapped on to the Europe/US divide. Not only does this ignore the complexities of global production and distribution, it also fails to correspond to changing aesthetic norms in different territories. To brand Amenábar as "Americanized" would be to surrender to Hollywood values of narrative dynamism and visual pleasure which are by no means alien to much popular European cinema today. The label "fine Continental fare" should not be restricted to art movies. Conversely to attack Crowe as a merchant of "sensationalist pap" would be to fail to respond to the particularity of his picture, whose aesthetic overload goes far beyond what is strictly necessary or, indeed, most effective for narrative exposition, the supposed goal of Hollywood. Arguably Crowe's media saturated sensibility, which remains more characteristic of New York than it is of Madrid, is highly appropriate for the two films' shared premise or concept: the hijacking of life by life extension, reality by virtuality. Certainly Cruise's star profile, based on hugely profitable good looks now threatened by age, makes the theme of male narcissism and disfigurement all the more pertinent. We have seen that the case of *Abre los ojos/Vanilla Sky* provoked high anxiety amongst filmmakers and audiences alike. But it also reveals with particular clarity the way in which the remake explores and intensifies that conflict between the formal and the industrial that remains central to cinema.

Works cited

Bourdieu, Pierre. *Distinction*. London: Routledge, 1996.

European Audiovisual Observatory. *Focus 2000: World Film Market Trends*. Cannes, 2001.

Fernández Santos, Elsa. 'Tom Cruise y Penélope Cruz dan la cara.' *El País* 27 January 2002, 34.

Fischer, Lucy. 'Modernity and postmaternity: *High Heels* and *Imitation of Life*.' In Horton and McDougal (1998), 200–16.

Forrest, Jennifer and Koos, Leonard R. (eds). *Dead Ringers: The Remake in Theory and Practice*. Albany, NY: SUNY Press, 2002.

Frater, Patrick and Kay, Jeremy. 'What makes a good remake?' *Screen International* 6 June 2003, 9.

Heredero, Carlos F. *Espejo de miradas*. Alcalá de Henares: Festival de cine, 1997.

—. *20 nuevos directores del cine español*. Madrid: Alianza, 1999.

Hopewell, John. 'Int'l success at last: sales push Spanish helmers beyond auteur status.' *Variety* 19–25 April 1999, 33, 40.

—. 'The gain in Spain ... falls mainly on a recent burst of hit local pix.' *Variety* 16–22 August 1999, 18.

Horton, Andrew and McDougal, Stuart Y. (eds). *Play It Again Sam: Retakes on Remakes*. Berkeley, CA: University of California Press, 1998.

Mazdon, Lucy. *Encore Hollywood: Remaking French Cinema*. London: BFI, 2000.

Naumann, Nils. 'Dos para la de Kidman.' *El País* 18 September 1999, 24.

Pérez Templado, Mariola. 'Película aburrida.' *ABC* 23 October 1999, 12.

Redbus. *Open Your Eyes* [pressbook]. London, 1999.

Sempere, Antonio. *Alejandro Amenábar: cine en las venas*. Madrid: Nuer, 2000.

SGAE. *Hábitos de consumo cultural*. Madrid: SGAE, 2000.

Shackleton, Liz, Rodier, Melanie and Zagt, Ab. 'All change again.' *Screen International* 6 June 2003, 11.

Smith, Paul Julian. *The Moderns: Time, Space, and Subjectivity in Contemporary Spanish Culture*. Oxford: Oxford University Press, 2000.

—. *Contemporary Spanish Culture: TV, Fashion, Art, and Film.*
   Cambridge: Polity, 2003.

Electronic sources

IMDb. Accessed 4 July 2003. www.IMDb.com
Lumiere. Accessed 10 October 2003.
   http://lumiere.obs.coe.int/web/EN/film_stats.php?film_id=
   12021
Ministerio de Cultura. Accessed 10 October 2003.
   www.cultura.mecd.es/cine/jsp/plantilla.jsp?id=131
Rotten Tomatoes. Accessed 10 October 2003.
   www.rottentomatoes.com/m/VanillaSky-1110491

Virtual Spain: Manuel Castells and Spanish web art

Castells in Spain

Hispanists continue to lament the exclusion of Spanish-speaking scholars from the international canon of cultural theory and the frequency with which English and French speaking theorists are cited within our own field. It is curious, then, that so little attention has been paid to the work of Manuel Castells, the global intellectual who has published some thirty books in as many years, charting the intersection of economics, society, and culture. The publication of the second edition of his synthetic masterpiece in three volumes, *The Information Age: Economy, Society and Culture* (Castells 2000), offers the opportunity to ask what Castells has to offer Hispanists.

Initially the neglect seems self-evident. In spite of his tendency to quote García Márquez and Neruda (most prominently, and in the Spanish original, at the climax to the fifteen hundred pages of his magnum opus), Castells seems insufficiently Spanish or Hispanic. Born in Spain, he trained and taught in Paris (beginning his career with the "events" of May 1968) before migrating to Berkeley, where he has officially been based since 1979. However, he has since then taught at some twenty universities around the world, including the Instituto de Sociología de Nuevas Tecnologías at the Autónoma in Madrid, the Universidad Mayor de San Simón, Cochabamba, Bolivia, and the UNAM in Mexico. More importantly, empirical analyses carried out by his research teams in these countries are, as we shall see, consistently integrated into his global vision. Hispanists can in this case no longer complain of their exclusion from theoretical studies which lay claim to general application.

The second reason for Castells' neglect is that, in spite of the term "culture" that is so prominent in the subtitle of his trilogy, he seems insufficiently cultural for those of us researching in the humanities. While indeed we will find little or no reference to literature in Castells' work and it abounds in statistics and graphs proclaiming its allegiance to the social sciences, it does however coincide with the current trend in Hispanism towards a cultural studies grounded in the particularity of location, as distinct from the now exhausted abstractions of "high theory." For example, Castells' account of the problematic intersection of global economics and local culture in the media enables us to place Spanish (Bolivian, etc.) audiovisual sectors in a global context. Moreover Castells' major thesis (namely that the technologized "network society" is inextricable from the birth of new identities) leads him to explore at length three fields that have received considerable attention in Hispanic studies over the last decade: gender, sexuality, and nationality. And while much of his synthetic overview may be dry and technical, he makes incursions into disciplines more familiar to the humanities, such as psychoanalysis; and with his almost lyrical account of "timeless time" and the "space of flows" comes close to a poetic vision of contemporary culture.

In the first half of this chapter I will offer a necessarily partial account of *The Information Age*, a project sometimes compared in its scale and ambition to Marx's analysis of the industrial era. I will then reread the work in a Hispanic key, isolating for analytic purposes, in a way Castells clearly does not encourage, the frequent and extended references to the Spanish (and indeed Catalan) speaking world. The second half of the chapter takes Castells as a matrix for the reading of two Spanish proponents of audiovisual web art. While Spain sometimes figures as an exception to the rule (and, strangely enough, is frequently juxtaposed with Japan), Castells' intimate familiarity with both Spain and Latin America also contributes substantially to his global vision of the intersection between technology and social movements: it is no surprise that Volume Two of his major work boasts on its cover a Zapatista mural from Chiapas.

Volume One (*The Rise of the Network Society*) is, as the title suggests, the most economically and technologically focused. Castells argues that "there [is] a fundamental split between abstract, universal instrumentalism and historically rooted, particularistic identities," or more concretely "a bipolar opposition between the Net and the self" (2000, Vol. 1, 3). Avoiding technological determinism, Castells traces in considerable detail a "revolution" that was "shaped" by late capitalism, but remains irreducible to the latter's interests (*ibid.*, 13) and whose specificity is "the action of knowledge upon knowledge" (17). Insisting on the social (and urban) context of technological change (*ibid.*, 59), Castells "demystifies the notion of placelessness ... in the Information Age" (67), arguing counter-intuitively for the persistence of the largest and oldest cities as centres for innovation (66). This tendency is in tension with a "networking logic" whose topography is decentred, flexible, and infinitely expandable (*ibid.*, 70–1). While the global economy can now for the first time "work as a unit in real time," "most production, employment, and firms remain ... local and regional" (*ibid.*, 101). Globalization and regionalization are thus "complementary" (*ibid.*, 111), even as "the uneven development of science and technology de-localizes the logic of informational production from its country basis and shifts it to multilocational, global networks" (129). The organizational shift is from "vertical bureaucracies to the horizontal corporation" (*ibid.*, 176) of the network enterprise, defined as "that specific form of enterprise whose system of means is constituted by the intersection of segments of autonomous systems of goals" (187). Just as the productive unit of new industries is no longer the individual or the collective but the network itself, in all its fluidity and interconnectedness, so the consumer audience of new media is "segmented, differentiated," rejecting simultaneity and uniformity" (*ibid.*, 368). In more imagistic terms, "we are not living in a global village, but in customized cottages globally produced and locally distributed" (*ibid.*, 370).

The social implications of this technological revolution are as follows: "widespread social and cultural differentiation," "increasing social stratification amongst users," "integration of all messages in a common cognitive pattern" (Castells 2000, Vol. 1, 402), and finally the "captur[ing] within [the] domain [of multimedia of] most cultural expressions, in all their diversity" (403). This "culture of real virtuality" finds its counterpart in the restructuring of urban space, in which cities are "increasingly differentiated in social terms, while being interrelated beyond physical contiguity" (*ibid.*, 433). New York and Mexico City are thus both globally connected and locally disconnected (*ibid.*, 436) in the space of flows that is constituted electronically through nodes and hubs (443). The counterpart of this disorientating space of flows is "timeless time." If modernity is conceived as "the dominance of clock time over space and society" (*ibid.*, 463), the information age is characterized by "arrhythmia" (475) in the life cycle of both work and reproduction (476); and in a simultaneity and discontinuity that lead to "systemic perturbation in the sequential order of phenomena" (494). Time and space are thus interdependent: "Timeless time belongs to the space of flows, while time discipline, biological time, and socially determined sequencing characterize places around the world" (*ibid.*, 495). Castells' example here is typically particular and resonant: the *cholular* business of Lima in which enterprising cell phone owners offer rental calls to people walking by in the street. It is an informal network enterprise offering "maximum flexibility in endless working days of unpredictable future" (*ibid.*, 495).

Volume Two, *The Power of Identity*, moves from technology to social movements. Castells initially divides identity into three categories: legitimizing (introduced by dominant institutions); resistance (generated by actors stigmatized by the logic of domination); and project ("build[ing] a new identity that redefines position[s] in society and [thus] seeks the transformation of overall social structure") (Castells 2000, Vol. 2, 8). While, historically, identities may change position amongst the three categories as they vary in relation to power, in general, legitimizing identity generates civil society; resistance leads to the formation of communes or communities; while project identity produces new subjects (*ibid.*, 9). Castells' argument is that "subjects, if and when constructed, are not built any longer on the basis of civil societies, that are in the process of disintegration, but as a prolongation of communal resistance" (*ibid.*, 11). Resistance to globalization is, however, by no means taken to be positive. Indeed, in the case of, say, Islamic fundamentalism, neo-community becomes "necro-community," in a peculiarly extreme and paradoxical form of violence (*ibid.*, 20). Rejecting the influential notion of "imagined communities" as "either obvious or empirically inadequate" (*ibid.*, 29), Castells claims that informational technologies "enhanc[e] our productive, capacity, cultural creativity, and communication potential ... at the same time [that they] disenfranchis[e] societies" (*ibid.*, 68–9). Similarly social movements contesting globalization are neither "bad" nor "good" in themselves, even as they share structural similarities: Castells' main examples here are the Zapatistas, the US militias, and the Japanese cultist Aum Shinrikyo (*ibid.*, 70). Such very diverse movements "surge from the depths of historically exhausted social forms, but decisively affect ...

the society in the making" (ibid., 108). The crisis of the patriarchal family is another example of "the interaction between structural change and social movements – that is between the network society and the power of identity" (ibid., 138). Castells relates the rise of feminism and of gay and lesbian movements to the formation of the advanced informational economy (ibid., 205). While there is no single new form of family, elements recur: "networks of support, increasing female-centeredness, succession of partners and patterns throughout the life-cycle" (ibid., 227). These new forms of sociability (which "de-link marriage, family, heterosexuality, and sexual expression" [ibid., 235]) are thus parallel, but not reducible, to the flexible, horizontal, and decentred businesses we saw in Volume One, which also reject "formal, institutionalized structure" (240).

The role of the media likewise challenges the autonomy and authority of the nation state through globalization of ownership, flexibility of technology, and the autonomy and diversity of the media themselves (Castells 2000, Vol. 2, 254). Typically, however, Castells stresses the rise of local and regional media, claiming this is as "important a trend as the globalization of media in shaping public attitudes" (ibid., 258). He also notes that there is a commercial incentive for broadcasters to be independent of national and industrial interests: "independence and professionalism ... translate into good business" (ibid., 257). Nation states, however weakened, are thus "not doomed to become an American colony" (ibid., 264); nor is the International Monetary Fund "an agent of American imperialism" (269). For in the US, as elsewhere, "what started as a process of re-legitimizing the state by shifting power from national to local level may end up deepening the legitimation crisis of the nation-state and [promoting] the tribalization of society in communities built around primary identities" (ibid., 275).

We have thus moved "from Big Brother to Little Sisters" (Castells 2000, Vol. 2, 299). While "statism disintegrated in contact with new information technologies" (ibid., 299), computers have processed a mass of individualized and personalized information in a kind of decentralized surveillance (301). Hence, although nation states will not disappear, they form increasingly "nodes of a broader network of power" (ibid., 304). Surveying the consequent "crisis of democracy," Castells denies that "media impose their political choices on public opinion" (*ibid.*, 311), arguing more subtly that there is a "framing of politics by their capture in the space of the media" (312), characteristic of the Information Age. This strategy, which may lead merely to the "politics of scandal," also enables resistance identities to play their part: "by inhabiting the space of media flows ... traditional cultures and popular interests assert their power" (*ibid.*, 333). Thus Castells concludes that while legitimizing identities "are drained away" (*ibid.*, 355), powerful resistance identities emerge but are unable to communicate with one another "except to struggle and negotiate on behalf of their specific interests/values" (356). Once more the "networking, decentered form of organization ... characteristic of new social movements" (as of the dominant informational society) makes innovative project identities heralding social change difficult indeed to identify (*ibid.*, 362).

The third and final volume, *End of Millennium*, rereads vast and diverse political changes in the light of the network enterprise. Thus the collapse of the Soviet Union reveals "the inability of statism to manage the transition to the Information Age" (Castells 2000, Vol. 3, 2). Castells shows how the (limited) Soviet introduction of computing proved only that "technological rationalization of social irrationality increases disorder" (*ibid.*, 37), as tension mounted between incompatible class and territorially based definitions of the state (41). Likewise the rise of the "Fourth World" of absolute poverty (in sub-Saharan Africa as in US ghettos) is a "structural outcome of trends embedded in informational capitalism when market forces remain unchecked" (*ibid.*, 129), namely inequality and social exclusion. Thirdly, the massive expansion of global crime in the 1990s is derived from "the flexibility and versatility of [its] organization" in which, no less than in the new technologies, "networking is the form of operation" (*ibid.*, 182). The global and the local intersect once more: "the more organized crime becomes global, the more its most important components emphasize their cultural identify, so as not to disappear in the whirlwind of the space of flows" (*ibid.*, 210).

The East Asian "developmental state," especially in Japan, reveals another example of the preservation of cultural identity or "modernizing without Westernizing" (Castells 2000, Vol. 3, 220). Rejecting both "[leftist] dogmatic dependency analysis and [rightist] neoclassical economics" (*ibid.*, 256), Castells shows how the Asian tigers achieved economic development under capitalism while employing "systematic state intervention" (258). It is however, the European Union that is the paradigm of the "network state" (*ibid.*, 339). Resulting haphazardly from differing defensive projects (or "Europe à la carte"), the "variable geometry of European construction, for all its incoherence, is an essential instrument of the construction itself, as it prevents frontal conflicts ... while allowing European institutions to muddle through the challenges presented by the two processes that ... further and oppose integration: economic globalization and cultural identity" (*ibid.*, 347). As Castells repeats, "a network, by definition, has nodes, not a center. Nodes may be of different sizes, and may be linked by asymmetrical relationships" (*ibid.*, 363). Unequal but interdependent, the various nodes of the EU do not preclude the building of a European project identity that would be "not in contradiction, but complementary to national, regional, and local identities" (*ibid.*, 365).

Castells thus concludes his three volumes by stressing once more the paradigm of network geometry "in which power relationships are always specific to a given configuration of actors and institutions" (Castells 2000, Vol. 3, 378) and "pattern[s] of social interaction [are] constructed, primarily, by the actual experience of the relationship" (380). While Castells warns repeatedly (and prophetically) that the interconnected nature of the network society makes its newly and uniquely vulnerable to "outright terror" ("a small determined group, well financed and informed, can devastate entire cities" [*ibid.*, 387]), his integrated analysis of economy, society, and culture remains open to "transformative political action" (389) of kinds that cannot be anticipated.

Before proceeding to my Hispanic rereading of Castells' project I would like to make three brief comments on the novelty and value of his method in cultural studies. First, in spite of its global reach and ambition, *The Information Age* is empirically based on primary research overseen by Castells in some twenty countries. In its meticulous documentation it thus avoids the theoretical abstraction of postmodernists, such as Baudrillard. Second, it is politically neutral. In spite of his transparent sympathy for those confined or consigned to the "black holes" of informational disconnection, Castells repeatedly stresses that "from an analytical perspective there are no progressive and regressive social movements" (e.g., Castells 2000, Vol. 2, 3) or, indeed, technologies. He thus avoids both the pessimism of technophobic Marxists, such as Jameson, and the utopianism of more recent uncritical advocates of cyberspace. Finally, he elaborates a new but not abstruse theoretical vocabulary that sidesteps exhausted debates on postmodernism and ideology alike, by positing the network as an analytical key to the homologous, but not identical or causally determined, fields of the economic, the social, and the cultural.

There is clearly a correspondence between the structure of the Spanish state and Castells' network paradigm, in which autonomous elements intersect, unequal yet interdependent. Moreover the resultant crisis of legitimacy of the state (often expressed in the politics of scandal) is wearisomely familiar. My own research on Spanish cultural industries suggests that Castells' general account of the media also holds for the particular case of Spain: Spanish cinema and television in the 1990s exhibited social and cultural stratification (a polarization between "quality" and trash programming); shrugged off US dominance by combining the global and the local; and revealed social attitudes relatively independent of even such heavy handed proprietors as Silvio Berlusconi (Smith 2000).

Castells himself had previously examined with his habitual collaborators the development of information technology in Spain. In the inappropriately named *España, fin de siglo* (published as early as 1992), he notes how the death of Franco in Madrid coincided with the birth of the personal computer in California (Alonso Zaldívar and Castells 1992, 181). In the decade that followed, while Spain grappled with modernity and democracy, more advanced nations were already transforming themselves into informational societies. Yet the new Spain is characterized by its openness to the new (*ibid.*, 183), and the Socialists doubled funding for research and development following the "Ley de la Ciencia" of 1986, albeit from a very low base (188). As a peripheral member of a central zone (Europe), Spain has not yet missed the boat: its combination of productive capacity and ability for improvisation and imagination may well save it (*ibid.*, 203). Ironically, perhaps, Castells also wrote shortly afterwards of a notable failure of Spain's decentred, network governance: the collapse of La Cartuja 93, the technopole or science city in Seville for which he himself had been the consultant (Castells and Hall 1994, 193–205).

To return to *The Information Age*, Castells' initial position in the first volume is that Spain's difference (like Japan's equally cited "uniqueness") will not fade away "in a process of cultural indifferentiation ... measured by rates of computer diffusion" (Castells 2000, Vol. 1, 20). Uneven development within states is illustrated with reference to the staggered industrial revolution in Spain, taking some hundred years to reach out from Catalonia (*ibid.*, 36). More recently the "horizontal" networking production pattern is found in footwear enterprises in Valencia (*ibid.*, 173), while a study of Spanish banking shows the "functional reintegration" of workers, retraining from being simple clerks to financial services salespeople (*ibid.*, 264). The same study found a "positive association between the introduction of information technology and employment" in Spain (*ibid.*, 275), refuting the commonplace that automation cost jobs. While Spain is "the worst performer in job creation," still it reduced unemployment by the end of the 1990s (*ibid.*, 279).

However, in this transformation of work, Spain is also the leader in a dominant trend: the increase in non-standard (i.e., casual or flexible) labour (Castells 2000, Vol. 1, 285). Spain is also particularly and suddenly open to Castells' "space of flows." The "backwater" of Madrid was transformed after 1986 by an influx of foreign capital which resulted in a real estate boom comparable to that of New York and London (*ibid.*, 411). The saturation of the inner core led to massive suburbanization and dislocation typical of the informational city: "an increase of disparities between the urban poles and their respective hinterlands" (*ibid.*, 411), even as the interdependency of far flung cities increased. Castells pays particular attention to Spanish architecture in this context. The "cold beauty" of Bofill's Barcelona airport ("an immense open space" panelled with glass [*ibid.*, 450], without carpeting or cosy rooms) exposes passengers to a "terrible truth: they are alone, in the middle of the space of flows ... they are suspended in the emptiness of transition" (451). Inversely Moneo's transformation of Madrid's old Atocha station into an indoor jungle, incongruously juxtaposed with the new high speed terminus, functions as a "broken mirror of a segment of the space of flows" (*ibid.*, 451). Castells juxtaposes a plan of the dense street network of Barcelona with one of the infrequent intersections of Irvine, the epitome of suburban southern California. While

Irvine "remains a place" it is one in which (unlike Barcelona) "the space of experience shrinks ... as flows take over increasing shares of time and space" (*ibid.*, 458).

If Spain is thus a peculiarly charged version of the network society, then it is also richly particular in its powers of identity, as Volume Two reveals. Castells gives an extended account of Catalonia as a paradigmatic "nation without a state" (Castells 2000, Vol. 2, 42–50). While much of this will be familiar to Hispanists, Castells' innovation is in relating this "differentiation between cultural identity and the power of the state" to the informational paradigm (*ibid.*, 50). Unlike nation states appealing to now shaky traditional notions of sovereignty, Catalan society is "based on flexibility and adaptability, a global economy, networking of media, [and] the variation and interpenetration of cultures" (*ibid.*, 50). Likewise Castells gives an extended account of the Zapatistas as one paradigmatic social movement resisting the new global order (*ibid.*, 72–83). It is not simply that the Zapatistas used "telecommunications, videos, and computer-mediated communication both to diffuse their messages from Chiapas ... and to organize a worldwide network of solidarity groups" (*ibid.*, 80). It is also that they understood that the "manipulation of information ... can be much more powerful than bullets" (*ibid.*, 81). While the relationship between this social movement and political institutions remained contradictory, the Zapatistas showed how "the new global order induces multiple local disorder, caused by historically rooted sources of resistance to the logic of global capital flows" (*ibid.*, 83).

Elsewhere, however, the Spanish-speaking world is taken to be anomalous. Thus Castells writes that "in most developed countries, with the major exceptions of Japan and Spain, the patriarchal family is in the process of becoming a minority form in the way people live" (Castells 2000, Vol. 2, 154–5). One parent households and births out of wedlock remain remarkably rare in Spain, compared to European or North American trends. Castells attributes this state not to Catholic moralism but rather to widespread youth unemployment and an acute housing crisis. He also notes that "the resistance of traditional patriarchal families in Italy and Spain takes its toll: women counteract by not having children, so that both countries are the lowest in the world in fertility rate, way below the replacement rate for the population" (*ibid.*, 152).

Not unrelated to this mixed message is Castells' account of Spanish feminism, which shows (he claims) "the potential of using politics and institutions to improve women's status, as well as the difficulty of remaining an autonomous social movement under conditions of successful institutionalization" (Castells 2000, Vol. 2, 191). The disappearance of a distinct feminist movement in Spain is contrasted with the apparent persistence of male bonding in "traditional patriarchal societies," of which Castells' example is the *peña* (*ibid.*, 234). Formerly reliant on female support safely corralled at home, such all-male social activities are transformed into "drinking mortuaries of male power" when women's status changes (*ibid.*, 234). Unskilled at "networking, solidarity, and relational skills" (*ibid.*, 233), men (and most especially Spanish men) are ill equipped for the more flexible familial models that are replacing patriarchalism.

The contemporary crisis of the nation state is represented by parallel histories of Mexico and the US Federal Government in the 1990s. How was it, asks Castells, that the PRI state, one of the most stable political regimes in the world, could disintegrate in just a few years? Castells claims that, in line with his global argument, it was because of "conflicts induced by the contradiction between globalization and identity" (Castells 2000, Vol. 2, 280). Undermined by the triple challenge of worldwide crime cartels, the Zapatista unmasking of national mythology, and a newly vibrant civil society (created in part, and ironically, by the PRI's tardy decentralization of power to states and cities), the Mexican state, like its northern neighbour, became "increasingly powerless" (*ibid.*, 286).

Castells' second volume finishes with two Hispanic examples of the crisis of democracy in the media. The first is the story of compadre Carlos Palenque of Bolivia, a folk musician of humble origin who became the owner of a media network and leader of a new political party (Castells 2000, Vol. 2, 329). While, for Castells, Bolivia, with its strong Indian identity and pervasive nationalism, would appear to be the "most likely country in the world to resist globalization of culture" (*ibid.*, 328), Palenque's electronic populism is "not dissimilar to the broader trends of informational politics [such as] the personalization of leadership; the simplification of messages ... the decisive importance of electronically broadcast language [and] the difficulty of fitting these new political expressions into traditional political categories" (*ibid.*, 332). Castells stresses that Palenque's populist programming in both TV and radio (which incorporates traditional elements and is addressed to the displaced poor) has a message, not just a medium, and cannot be reduced to "media manipulation" (*ibid.*, 331). It is only, however, by "inhabiting the space of media flows" that such cultures can assert themselves, while being transformed in the process (*ibid.*, 333). Castells' second example is corruption scandals in the Spain of the 1980s and 1990s. While the details of successive PSOE scandals will be depressingly familiar to many Spanish specialists, what matters is Castells' analytic account of why and how they took place when they did. While not denying that there was "a significant level of corruption" in the Socialist government, Castells claims that what is important is "the use of scandal politics in and by the media as the fundamental weapon utilized by political actors, business interests, and social groups to fight one another" (*ibid.*, 341). If politics is "captured" in the space of the media, it also responds unpredictably to a network paradigm in which multiple factors, including the press and judiciary, feed off one another symbiotically (*ibid.*, 338). Comparing the Spanish situation to the Italian (in which Berlusconi's commercial dominance did not save him from continuous scandal), Castells concludes that "overwhelming business influence in the media is not tantamount to political control in informational politics," because "in scandal politics, as in other domains of the network society, the power of flows overwhelms the flows of power" (*ibid.*, 342).

Turning to Castells' final volume, we find that Spain and Portugal do not bear out the "structural trend toward increasing inequality in the network society," blessed as they still are with "stable, moderate inequality" (Castells 2000, Vol. 3, 80). Inversely Colombian *narcotráfico* exhibits all the signs of Castells' global-local hybridity. It is a uniquely "Latin American controlled, export-oriented industry, with proven global competitiveness" (*ibid.*, 200), that has reversed the pattern of dependency. However, narrating his visits to Bolivia, Peru, and Colombia (where he observed the contrast between luxury consumer goods and devastated infrastructure), Castells denies that drug trafficking is developmental, as financial benefits are offset by violence and instability (*ibid.*, 202). Decentred and flexible, "occupying for the first time a hegemonic position in a major sector of the global economy," drug networks reveal nonetheless "the importance of cultural identity in [their] constitution, functioning, and strategies" (*ibid.*, 202). Ironically enough, the dynamic is not so different to that of Spain within the European Union. On the one hand Spain wishes "to be anchored in a strong unified Europe" in order to "prevent the country from returning to the demons of political authoritarianism and cultural isolationism" (*ibid.*, 342); on the other hand, as a "pluri-national state" Spain displays a "retrenchment around the principle of national identit[ies]" (*ibid.*, 360). The EU is thus caught between "the high winds of globalization and the warm hearth of locality" (*ibid.*, 361).

We have seen, then, that Castells appeals to Spain and Latin America, no less than to Japan and Russia, in order to illustrate his theme of the net and the self. And if Spanish-speaking countries alternately confirm and deny the general trends Castells identifies, this is consistent with a flexible theory that seeks to account for a technological revolution that has both united the world's economies into a single, simultaneous mechanism and splintered the world's societies into multiple, non-reciprocal identities. Indeed Castells' final lament, answered only by an enigmatic poem from Neruda, is that "there is an extraordinary gap between our technological overdevelopment and our social underdevelopment" (Castells 2000, Vol. 3, 390). As Castells has written elsewhere, Spaniards who in their everyday life continue to disregard the discipline of clock time associated with a now outmoded industrial modernity (Alonso Zaldívar & Castells 1992, 68–9) may be better placed than most to cope with the newly arrhythmic "timeless time" of the space of flows. Certainly the burgeoning field of Spanish electronic art deserves closer study, reworking as it does in typically fluid form Castells' themes of work and pleasure, nationality and nomadism. *The Information Age* thus offers Hispanists a unique opportunity to rethink the relation between culture and identity in the many customized cottages of our own discipline.

The net and the self

As Castells has noted, in spite of its love of novelty, contemporary Spain is not known for its embrace of new technologies. It is thus particularly important to pay attention to those few pioneers of electronic art who have, to my knowledge, received little notice abroad. I have chosen in the second half of this chapter to analyse two major figures, teasingly similar yet distinctly different. Marisa González, born in Bilbao, has worked on the interface between art and technology for some thirty years. Leaving late Francoist Spain for Chicago in the early 1970s she embraced the collective project Generative Systems, headed by the Art Institute's Sonia Sheridan (Sheridan 2000, 43). Her career has taken her from mail and fax art to digitally manipulated still photography, installations, and accompanying websites. Albert (or Alberto or Tito) Porta took the name Zush when temporarily interned in Barcelona's Phrenopathic Hospital. Caught up like González with the social movements of the 1960s (although, in his case, not the Vietnam War protests but the hippy lifestyle), Zush has created and elaborated his own imaginary State, complete with language and script, over three decades (Ullán and Zush 2000). Like González, he has exploited a range of media, both traditional (painting and analogue photography) and novel (a prize winning CD-ROM and an elaborate website).

While the habitus of the two artists could hardly be more different, with González exploiting the impersonality of technological reproduction and Zush inventing a unique, indeed idiosyncratic, universe, I will argue that in their shared commitment to new technologies they embody what Castells calls the "information age." Both artists constitute advanced "network enterprises," in Castells' formulation, in relation to production and consumption. González was actually named "network" representative in Spain by her teacher and generative systems inventor Sheridan. And her work has grown unpredictably from interaction with international correspondents and local technicians. Zush, an archetypal "outsider artist" who is surrounded with an aura of individual mystique, collaborated early on with British musician Peter Gabriel in the production of digitally generated imagery for a pop video (*Digging in the Dirt*, 1992); and his current works feature (like those of González) extensive technical credits, acknowledging his assistants. There is thus in both a certain tension between the traditional uniqueness of the artist and the collaborative enterprise of the information era or, in Castells' terms once more, between the historical rootedness of identities and the abstract universalism of the Web.

This conflict between the self and the net is particularly acute here in the case of artists who originate in the "historic nationalities" of the Basque Country and Catalonia, continue to work mainly in the shifting network states of Spain and the EU, and yet are are globally distributed. The transformations of time and space effected by and in the information age thus register acutely in González and Zush's artistic practice, as, arguably, they do in the unevenly developed and decentred Spanish state.

However, while Spanish critics have tended to read both artists in postmodern terms (with reference to, say, Baudrillard's "simulacrum" or Vattimo's "aesthetic of disappearance") (e.g., Gras Balaguer 2000, 25), they have failed to address that interconnection of economy, society, and culture that Castells has so brilliantly and exhaustively demonstrated. As we shall see, the network society gives birth to new and strange identities, captured in the shifting spaces of digital technology. It is perhaps no accident that the summer of 2000 saw major exhibitions by both artists in Madrid, thus establishing their place at the centre of the Spanish national art world even as they were disseminated globally through their websites.

Marisa González: the dream factory

González is clearly well aware of academic debate on new technologies. In an "address" or "call" (*convocatoria*) for a piece called "Fax Station" (1993–95), in which international artists sent works that were printed on to an endless roll suspended in the central stairwell of Madrid's monumental Círculo de Bellas Artes, she writes that her aim is not to create a tangible, mercantile object but rather to create a dialogue, or "multidirectional information" (González 2000, unpaginated). Technical means serve thus to "alter space and time," rendering the first "continuous" and the second "instantaneous."

Set against this networking logic, decentred, flexible, and multiple, González's more recent project *La fábrica* (*The Factory*) seems an aberration (Figures 15, 16). Funded by Telefónica, Spain's multinational communications giant, and exhibited at its grandiose headquarters on Madrid's Gran Vía, *La fábrica* derives from a distinct, indeed unique, event and location: the destruction of a massive industrial bakery that had stood for a century in the heart of Bilbao. González combines multiple media, in addition to the website, also hosted by Telefónica, to which visitors are encouraged to contribute. Large scale still photographs (the biggest 125 x 165 cm) are displayed thematically: the *fachadas* (facades) focus on the seven massive silos, visual logo of the project; *derribo* (tearing down) documents the destruction of the factory, with massive concrete blocks suspended like beads on a string and railway lines plunging into the void; *artefactos* and *interiores* show gaily coloured tubing or menacing metal spirals, enigmatically and inexplicably deprived of use value; finally, *cubiertas de agua* (water roofs) show digitally "unfolded" or treated images of the cooling pools on the roof of the factory, endlessly extended and surprisingly rural vistas of reflecting water and flourishing vegetation. Bilbao's familiar hills unfold, repeatedly, in the misty background.

These uncanny photos (whose seamless digital manipulation is not at first apparent) are contrasted with complex installations. "Silo" consists of an original artifact rescued from the site: inside it is transformed into a perilous human habitation, decked with yellowing documents and watched over by an aging clock. In "Luminarias" ("Lamps") ominous ranks of black lamps (also retrieved from the doomed site) project on to the floor texts taken from management files discovered by González: they document the disciplining of the workers (from the management fear of strikes in the 1910s through Fascist exaltation of the "battle of grain" in the 1930s, to praise of *informatización* as control of the workforce in the 1960s). Labour life is juxtaposed, pathetically, with domesticity: identity cards of long lost workers, complete with photos and personal details, are projected onto the wall behind. Finally, a tripartite video installation deafeningly protracts and repeats the final fall of the factory, seen from different angles and at different speeds.

Clearly González, who denies her work implies "retro" antiquarianism or melancholy (Gras Belaguer 2000, 14), is documenting, beyond discrete particularity, the fall of the industrial era as a time-space complex. As the industrial city par excellence, Bilbao is one of the few places in Spain to have suffered the full rigours of modernity. Abandoned and empty, this very particular place becomes grotesque, its endless admonishments to absent workers (not to enter or smoke, to park their vehicles and measure their materials correctly) more pathetic than tragic. Moreover the enigmatic remains, implicitly reappropriated by González, become unstably aestheticized: primary coloured tubes invoke the Pompidou Centre, scribbled blackboards Josef Beuys, and spiral metal contraptions the

Louise Bourgeois also cited by González's curator (Gras Belaguer 2000, 33). While González painstakingly documents the specific time-space practices of a century's labour (paying her respects to the ghostly workers whose identity cards are briefly projected on the gallery wall), she also appropriates and distorts that practice. The discipline of clock time is betrayed by the endless repetition of the monstrous, falling silos. And the constrictions of industrial space are opened out in the "unfolding" landscapes of the placid pools, where reflections recur unpredictably and uncannily. In the words of González's curator and exegete, the particular physiognomy of "place" is converted into the "territory" of the artist's performance (*actuación*), which is itself "another space" (*ibid.*, 32). Moreover the traditional ontology of the photographic image, as trace of the real, is subtly undermined, even as González mourns and memorializes the lost referent.

La fábrica thus employs digital technology to recreate the arrhythmic timeless time and the disorientating space of flows which Castells takes to be the most important characteristics of the network paradigm. But still it appeals implicitly to the power of identity. Significantly, the only interactive activity permitted by the accompanying website was a call for surfers to submit photos of abandoned factories in their own vicinity, accompanied by text describing their own experience or memory of these empty spaces. Responses testified more directly than González's relatively oblique treatment to the persistent personal investment in institutional or industrial architecture. In the interview printed in the catalogue, moreover, González claims the factory is both symbolic of Basque industry and "inseparable" from her own biography (Gras Belaguer 2000, 11). Critics also read her work, apparently impersonal, as subjective and imaginative. The curator claims it reveals the co-existence of the most sophisticated technology with the "pathology" of aesthetic feeling, a contradiction derived from a "split self." Moreover digitalization of photography introduces a "subjectivization" of images taken from reality. Another critic writes in the catalogue that González, in accompanying the "fall" of reality, strikes a "heroic testimonial" note (Castro 2000, 73). While any individualistic reference to the material deprivation of life under Franco can only be inferred (just as the symbolic charge of bread as staff of life is only implicit), the trace of the body in now empty space is strongly felt.

González calls her successive journeys through the desolate factory *recorridos*, implying (unlike the English translation, given as "routes") the subject's trajectory through territory. As in Bourgeois, again, there is also an implied association between building and body: the wounded silos gape with semicircular openings like eyes or lips; a windowless grey metal box is labelled "Celda no. 10" ("Cell no. 10"), as if awaiting an industrial anchorite. And if *La fábrica* is rigorously devoid of human figures, González's previous work did not avoid allusion to humanoid forms, investing objects with subjective life: mutant rotting lemons echo female genitalia; disjointed dolls suggest rape (Gras Belaguer 2000, 13).

The persistence of identity in González is thus not simply local, narrating the brutality of Basque industrialization; it is also implicitly gendered, as in the celebration of González's collaboration with her *maestra* Sonia Sheridan (see Maderuelo 1998). The disappearance of the working class is also perhaps that of the patriarchal family: the ghostly couples branded as *matrimonios* ("husbands and wives") in the factory's identity cards. González's more flexible digital practice, the operation of information on information, thus points mutely to new project identities, particularly those based on a female genealogy, held by Castells to be characteristic of the information age.

On consulting the website, however, González's innovations seem more modest. Digital rain (stereotypical of damp Bilbao) falls over the still photos of the facades; a green text absent in the exhibition (announcing that the "contemporary revolution" is "uncertainty") drifts over the monochrome instructions to industrial employees. The massive silos, curiously weightless and two dimensional here, fall successively from the screen to reveal the waterscapes. Newly prominent is the clock. Confined in the exhibition to the silo installation, here it floats over the static non-smoking signs, looming up and pulling back from the digital viewer, exploiting the freedom of movement and scale on screen. A new slogan, perhaps over explicit, points out or pins down the clock's significance: "El reloj parado, retención del tiempo" ("The stopped clock: the holding back of time"). The clock face also floats over the interactive *convocatoria*. On 14 February 2002, some eighteen months after the exhibition was inaugurated, twenty-two participants had submitted their own spaces and texts. In spite of potentially global access, however, it is clear that the attraction of the site was local: twenty of these were from Spaniards in Spain, while one Spanish exile added a resonant and relevant urban location: the Nazi-built former Spanish consulate, still ruinous in the new Berlin. The only US contributor bears a familiar name: it is Sonia Sheridan, González's Chicago mentor. González's relatively timid excursions into multimedia (ghostly choirs sing over the factory's ruins) are thus in tune with her audience's continuing attachment to pre-modern locality, a preference characteristic of Spain's decentred network state. As *La fábrica* shows so richly, the fall of the industrial era does indeed not only lead to informational flow; it also renders once objectively disciplined spaces vulnerable to subjective identification and uncontrolled fantasy.

Perhaps like her nostalgic and provincial web partners, González, the digital pioneer, is ambivalent also about new technologies. In interview she claims that what she once felt was the "poetics" of technology has now become a "vertigo." And while formerly she was pigeonholed as "high tech," now she is said to be "low tech." Loyal to outdated visualizing systems devised and promoted by her teachers of Generative Systems, she has resisted recent developments, often preferring to take analogue photographs of images on digital screens (Gras Belaguer 2000, 16). As in her attachment to material objects, gathered laboriously and even dangerously on site, González here exhibits a kind of archaizing nostalgia for artistic uniqueness and a suspicion of reproductive technology that outruns its subject matter. Recycling the industrial era, dislocating its ordered space and confounding its clock time, González launches the *La fábrica* website enthusing over the Web as interactivity, communication, and virtual community (*ibid.*, 18). Yet her lengthy and impressive commitment to global collaboration is in tension with the Web's necessarily abstract instrumentalism and cannot be separated from her quest for newly particular identities which pass through the body. As she wrote in a text of 1996, significantly called "Identidad territorios" ("Identity Territories"): "localizar los deseos, fabricar los sueños,/ reinventar el yo y el otro, inventar una nueva utopía" ("Localize desires, fabricate dreams,/ reinvent the self and other, invent a new utopia") (González, *Fragmentos*). The reconstruction of identity is thus at once facilitated and precluded by the utopian promise of new technologies.

Zush: real virtuality

If González has explored the time based artistic practice of Generative Systems and reappropriated concrete locations in the abstract space of the Web, Zush has created his own apparently autonomous artistic universe of wilfully anachronistic timeless time and a disconcertingly mobile space of flows. And González's apparent impersonality could not be more different from Zush's flagrant solipsism, so typical of what Castells calls the "real virtuality" of multimedia. In an obsessively repeated iconography and graphology, Zush thus reconfirms the hermetic isolation typical of the outsider artist, particularly one with a history of mental illness (Figures 17, 18). Recurrent visual motifs (all derived from physiology) include eyes (often embedded directly in brains); genitals (including explicit, if mutilated, polaroids of penetration); and distorted and manipulated faces and figures (whether human or animal). This personalized image repertoire is explored in minutely disturbing detail and volume: Zush has produced thousands of graphic works in ink, paint, nail varnish, or collage that refuse reduction to the curatorial formula: "mixed media on paper." And if he boasts the most sophisticated website and CD-ROM of any Spanish artist, he has also specialized (as Antonio Monegal has noted) in that most unique and material of media: the one-off artist's book (Monegal 2000).

Most challenging and off-putting in its privacy is Zush's elaboration of a new language (Asura) for his private state of Evrugo. The runic traces of Evrugo (reminiscent, as the name suggests, of cursive Hebrew script; derived in fact from simplified Latin characters) swarm and proliferate throughout Zush's works, revealing the horror vacui also thought to be characteristic of outsider artists. There is a compulsive repetition here that reveals not only the insistence of the handmade letter (with the scribe endlessly reiterating his personal mark), but also the archaism of Zush's techno-utopia (a painstaking practice which predates mechanical repetition). A new found, ancient civilization, Evrugo is testimony to an archeology of the future, in which Zush's graphic traces call into being that realm of ecstatic pleasure which, playfully, they claim to document. On the cover of the catalogue to Zush's great retrospective exhibition, held at the prestigious Reina Sofía, is a stylized and alarmed face (mouth agape, eyes swiveling) drawn in the shape of a bell (the exhibition was called *La campanada* ["the bell stroke or chime"]). Covered in tiny dots, a persistent indicator of Zush's individual, indeed manual, attention, it floats on a background of handwritten Asuran characters, extended as if to infinity beyond the edge of the page.

The exhibition staged further, albeit ironic, references to Zush's hermetic exclusivity. The opening room featured an Evrugo flag (eye on brain) fluttering proudly in the air conditioning, standing guard over the meticulously produced currency (tucares) which won Zush an award for innovation in printing. Stamps and passports (punning on Zush's real name: "Pasa, Porta") complete the collection. Inside, long corridors of graphic works revealed Zush's love of seriality, ironically customized by his handmade practice. The series of playing cards distort and contort the ready made iconography of both esoteric Tarot and localist Spanish packs. Most singular of all was the temporary habitation built in the final gallery of the exhibition: at (unspecified) times Zush promised to live and work in this provisional space, a full scale translucent studio fully equipped with both the high and low tech tools (computers and nail varnish) that go to make up a private universe.

The practice of everyday life is thus incorporated unstably and unpredictably into the esoteric abstraction of Evrugo and the Web. Spectators disappointed by the physical Zush's absence were reduced to playing with the ever ready CD-ROM, projected giant scale on to the gallery wall. Here Zush (aided by his technical team and Peter Gabriel's evocative electronic music) exploits the potential of new media as obsessively as he had the old. Initially a rational, discursively articulated structure seems clear. Just as González's "generative strategies" direct and subtend her time based projects and the seven silos logo visually articulates *La fábrica*, so Zush's title *Psico-Manual-Digital* appears to inform and contain his slippery space of flows. Clicking on the initial cat-like biomorph reveals a tripartite screen with icons (brain, finger, and computer mouse) labelled in English, Spanish, and Asura. Further investigation reveals uncharacteristic chunks of written text in which the psychic is defined (after Gurdjieff) as "transpersonal memory," the manual (after Fritz Lang) as a "bridge" or "tool," revealing that the author of the text is language itself; and finally the Web is defined as an "exogamous brain" or (after an anachronistic Foucault) a "technology of the self." This rationalization of a wilfully idiosyncratic project reveals not only that Zush (like González) is not indifferent to academic appropriation of his art; it also suggests a metatextual objectivity that transcends the hermeticism of multimedia, which, as Castells writes, reduces all signals to a single message.

Typically, however, this unique and weighty wedge of text is set against the anonymous and urgent demands of the body: a soundtrack of panting sends the spectator clicking back to the previous screen. The dazzling, vertiginous graphics here seem indistinguishable, whether one choses brain, hand, or mouse: cut up bodies (reminiscent of the Surrealist exquisite corpses) chop and change; swirling masks or faces morph into each other or graphic nudes boasting Zush's trademark eyeball heads. Psyche, tool, and technology are cut and shuffled here like playing cards. Moreover the section titled "Asura" blurs another basic distinction: that between image and text, iconography and graphology. A too rapid flashing of Zush's phosphorescent humanoid figures gives way to a blinking display of Asura text, black on red. But if text is image (the invented alphabet stands revealed as both decoration and computer code), then Zush's disorientating "pleasure bomb" (a repeated phrase from the soundtrack) is also a subtle pedagogic device. The home screen of the website invites us to press our keyboard: appropriate Asuran characters appear on the backdrop (the pulsating circle of a chromosome or planet). The CD-ROM goes further with a translation facility, whereby everyday English or Spanish words are transmutated into the exotic garb, at once archaic and novel, of Zush's increasingly familiar private script. Likewise choosing "Zush" from the main menu enables the initiate to customize the opening image (a one-eyed biomorph) by varying colour, background, and features. Infinitely fluid, still it remains, however, recognizably Evrugan. In spite of its multiplicity and fluidity, then (and its generous and genuine invitation to collaborate, so different to *La fábrica*), Zush's electronic work retains a proud solipsism and an artistic singularity as distinct as a signature, whether it is inscribed in Spanish or Asuran.

But just as González's resonant absences (the ghostly trace of workers and spectators in the dream factory) subjectivize her impersonal locations, so, inversely, Zush's all too voluble and visible projections (the massed words and images of Evrugo) ultimately

objectify his personal trajectory. Or to put it another way, the particularity of Spanish territory and history inflects both of these virtual projects in unpredictable ways. González's Bilbao childhood is
"inseparable" from the bakery, however abstracted in her work; similarly Zush's early life in Barcelona is contaminated by the eccen-
tricities of his later work, retrospectively subjected to the "Evrugo
Mental State." Personal photos reproduced in the catalogue (of the
child Tito in school smock posed in front of a Spanish map, mas-
querading as a flamenco dancer with a youthful companion, and
sweetly angelic at his First Communion) testify to a Francoist Spain
that is now more remote and bizarre from the contemporary state
than any invented cyber-utopia.

Indeed Zush's Pyrrhic or Sisyphean labour in establishing and
elaborating a self-sufficient State (complete with national anthem)
is concurrent with and perhaps parodic of the Catalan *autonomía*
which has developed over the same decades. When faced with the
violent and overdetermined choice between Catalan or Castilian,
Asuran seems a reasonable alternative, particularly when compared to the English that has been adopted as a lingua franca by
many web artists based in Catalonia. The Zush who labels his works
indifferently in all four languages thus celebrates a flow that is not
merely spatial, exploiting the flexibility of digital media, but is also
linguistic and cultural. It is perhaps no accident that none of the
texts in the Madrid catalogue make the uncomfortable connection
between Evrugo and Catalonia, favouring as they do more abstract
discourses on the autonomy of the aesthetic.

Following Castells, once more, we might read Zush's art, with its
substantial logistical resources and relative commercial success, as
an emblematic network enterprise for both Catalonia, the frontier
nation, and Spain, the network state. For an outsider artist, Zush has
powerful protectors overseas (including Peter Gabriel) and, unlike
Marisa González, he has embraced all technological advances,
enthusing over the increasing speed with which images can be
scanned, distorted, and reproduced. He has even incorporated into
his practice with mordant irony the economy of the art market:
when works are exchanged for cash, why should the artist not sim-
plify the process by printing his own money, the notes embossed
with a typically mutated Evrugan head? (see González García
2000). And a chirpy electronic voice on the CD-ROM announces

that, on receipt of cheque or money order, Zush will supply lucky consumers with a "pleasure bomb." If the network enterprise is characterized by ceaseless and instantaneous "horizontal" development (rather than discrete and sequential "vertical" hierarchy) then the genealogies and geographies of Evrugo, an informational universe that is digitally distributed, are perhaps the closest Spain has come to a cultural equivalent of Silicon Valley.

Art after privatization

One consequence of the decline of the nation state, amply documented by Castells, is the crisis in cultural heritage. Just a few months after González's exhibition had closed in the Telefónica's temporary gallery, *El País* reported that the Ministry of Culture was attempting to retrieve the company's precious permanent collection (featuring major works by Gris, Chillida, Tàpies, and Picasso) lost to public ownership when Telefónica had been privatized some four years earlier (Argos 2001). The Reina Sofía (site of Zush's exhibition) had recommended the collection be retained because of its "quality and representativity," which could not be recreated given the prices such works now commanded. Telefónica was asked to surrender a Juan Gris in lieu of taxes. The legitimation crisis in the economic, social, and cultural spheres associated with the waning of the nation state has rarely been so clearly revealed. Zush's conceptual currency (the "tucares") was thus outstripped by the transparent mercantilism embodied in the most prestigious of traditional artworks.

Zush's virtual gallery (in which, guided by the mouse, the surfer squints up at works hanging mutely on cyber-walls), apparently the least ambitious of his electronic spaces, might thus be read as a vindication of a public art space only recently abandoned in the real Spain. Likewise his apparently aggressive solipsism (caustically figured by the creature called "Fuckface:" a beast endlessly penetrating its own orifice) might better be read in a social context as a critique of such phenomena as the the splintering of societies and cities into non-communicative fragments. As Castells has written, analysis is not to be confused with advocacy. And if Zush's topographic model is the sphere (revolving celestial and corporeal orbs) then this need not imply hermetic circularity. Rather the labyrinthine Evrugo is a network society in which decentred but interconnected nodes constantly collide. González's geometry is more linear, like the endless fax rolls with which she once experimented. On her website, however (still hosted by Telefónica in 2004), the blank facades and empty interiors suggest (as Bofill's and Moneo's architecture did to Castells) that we are suspended in the emptiness of transition, caught in the space of flows. While Zush suggests new project identities, profiting from the polymorphous pleasure bomb of the Web, González points perhaps to a identity that resists the new law of uncertainty, but one based only on necro-community or social exclusion: the long lost workers whose IDs flash briefly and successively on the gallery wall. This co-existence of the real and the virtual, dependent on a radically new electronic order, is not perhaps without structural antecedents. For Freud, also, fantasy was barely and only intermittently distinguishable from psychic reality (Laplanche and Pontalis 1988, s.v. "phantasy").

For Castells the network geometry, whether found in a firm or a family, is immanent: power relations are specific to a given configuration of actors and institutions and social interactions are constructed by the actual experience of the relationship. The "customized cottages" of González and Zush testify not only to the persistence of location, whether historical or fantastic, in a time of supposed placelessness. They also suggest that while transcendence is no longer feasible (no Marxism to nourish the bread workers, no psychiatry to correct or console the Evrugan mutants), translatability is still possible. Zush's appeal to the linguistic paradigm of structuralism (in which it is language itself that speaks in the text) can thus be reread for the information age. In virtual Spain, electronic pioneers have shown that the intersection of autonomous elements (of art as of the state) can produce new cultural, social, and even economic forms.

Works cited

Alonso Zaldívar, Carlos, and Castells, Manuel. *España, fin de siglo*. Madrid: Alianza, 1992.

Argos, Lucía. 'El arte después de las privatizaciones: Cultura quiere recuperar obras de la Colección Telefónica a cambio del pago de impuestos.' *El País* 4 March 2001, 31.

Castells, Manuel. *The Information Age, Volume 1: The Network Society*. Oxford: Blackwell, 2000.

—. *The Information Age, Volume 2: The Power of Identity*. Oxford: Blackwell, 2000.

—. *The Information Age, Volume 3: End of Millennium*. Oxford: Blackwell, 2000.

—, and Peter Hall. *Technopoles of the World: The Making of Twenty-First-Century Industrial Complexes*. London: Routledge, 1994.

Castro, Fernando. 'Fragmentos de la memoria.' In González 2000, 70–5.

González, Marisa. *La fábrica: registros hiperfotográficos e instalaciones* [catalogue]. Madrid: Fundación Telefónica, May–June 2000. Curated by Menene Gras Balaguer.

González García, Angel. 'Donde una vez más se habla de dinero.' In Zush 2000, 61–76.

Gras Belaguer, Menene. 'La fábrica: conversación.' In González 2000, 11–21.

—. 'Destrucción: retórica del simulacro en función de lo sublime.' In González 2000, 25–39.

Laplanche, J. and Pontalis, J. B. *The Language of Psychoanalysis*. London: Karnak, 1988.

Maderuelo, Javier. 'Sobre el sexo de la tecnología.' *El País: Babelia* 4 July 1998.

Monegal, Antonio. 'Lo sagrado del libro. Evrugo encuadernado.' In Zush 2000, 273–80.

Sheridan, Sonia. 'Sistemas generativos.' In González 2000, 43–9.

Smith, Paul Julian. 'Spanish quality TV? The *Periodistas* notebook.' *Journal of Spanish Cultural Studies* 1, 2000, 173–91.

Ullán, José Miguel and Zush. 'Biografía autorizada.' In Zush 2000, 13–19.

Zush. *La campanada* [catalogue]. Madrid: Museo Nacional Centro de Arte Reina Sofía, June–August 2000. Curated by José Miguel Ullán.

Electronic sources

González, Marisa. *La fábrica*. Accessed 17 March 2004. www.fundacion.telefonica.com/at/lafabrica/lafabrica/intro_menu.html

—. 'La fábrica: registros hiperfotográficos e instalaciones.'
   Accessed 17 March 2004.
   http://w3art.es/magonzal/fabrica.htm
—. *Fragmentos*. Accessed 17 March 2004. www.marisa-gonzalez.
   com/fragmentos.html
Mubimedia and Zush. *Psico-Manual-Digital*. CD-ROM, 1997.

8 Transatlantic traffic in recent Hispano-Mexican films

Between Spain and Mexico: the question of co-production

In this final chapter I consider the recent resurgence of Mexican cinema (praised from *Kinetoscopio* to the *The Economist*) as a test case for Manuel Castells' theory of "the interaction between technology-induced globalization, the power of identity (gender, religious, national, ethnic, territorial, socio-biological), and the institutions of the state" (Castells 2000, 2). Focusing on relations between Mexico and Spain, I examine the various and overlapping regulatory regimes which still frame audiovisual production in Europe and Latin America; address the increasingly powerful commercial dimension by offering corporate studies of two innovative Mexican producers, Altavista and Anhelo; and, finally, give an account of the two best known films in the so-called renaissance: *Amores perros* (2000) and *Y tu mamá también* (2001). While these two famous features are not technically co-productions (and indeed have been praised for their sense of locality) I argue that they participate in a newly intense economic and cultural exchange between Latin America and Europe through the transatlantic reach of their parent companies (Compañía Iberoamericana de Entretenimiento [CIE] and Omnilife, respectively [electronic sources]) and their idiosyncratic casting of Spanish actresses in central roles.

The last two years have seen frequent, if contradictory, accounts in the trade press of this Ibero-American traffic, in which Hollywood is often a third corner in a golden triangle. In its annual survey published in its 24 December 2001 issue, *Variety* wrote that "Homegrown pix gain[ed] in Europe," especially in Spain where market share increased from 10% to 19%. However, the true picture was more complex. Much of this gain was due to a film branded a "hybrid:" Alejandro Amenábar's English speaking *The Others*. And the production boom remained "extremely fragile" with many of the 91 theatrically released Spanish features disappearing without trace. Corporate moves in all directions also complicated the scene. Telefónica Media, a division of the Spanish communications giant based in Miami, took control of leading Spanish producer LolaFilms, aiming to "transform it into a major content creator and provider for the international Spanish-speaking market" (*Screen International* 26 November 1999). Meanwhile Sony "beef[ed] up Spanish production," aiming to make films in Spain and in Spanish "primarily for the local market but [also to] be distributed overseas" (*Screen International* 28 September 2001). Sogecable (which co-produced "box-office phenomenon" *The Others* with Tom Cruise) "started an international drive" to back "more ambitious projects" (*ibid.*). Meanwhile "Spanish [producers] eye[d] up US suitors" (12 October 2001) as Sony was joined by Buena Vista International in co-producing local films in Spain. The attraction here was once more the transatlantic connection. "Latin America," writes *Screen International*, "is a huge secondary market which makes Spanish-language films potentially more lucrative than German- or French-language product" (*ibid.*). One executive cautions that "films made in Spain do not easily translate to the Spanish-speaking world," but still confirms that the Latin American market is "an added lure." The gendered or eroticized language here ("suitors," "lure") is not infrequent in such commercial contexts. Festivals joined in the transatlantic love affair. In 2001 San Sebastián gave its major prize to a Latin American feature for the third time in four years (*ibid.*). The 17th Muestra de Cine Mexicano in Guadalajara repaid the compliment with a large Spanish selection ("Cine por la red," 27 February 2002).

Focus 2000, the annual survey of the industry produced by the Strasbourg based European Audiovisual Observatory (2000), gives a more nuanced picture at the start of the millennium. Spanish feature production peaked at 91 in 1995 before declining to 65 in 1998 and rising to 82 in 1999. Underlying these figures, however, is a steeper decline in "100% national" films and a consistent increase in co-productions, from 25 to 36 in the same period. Cinema admissions also continued their steady rise, almost doubling during the course of the 1990s from 78 million to 131 million. Market share for 1999 is given as: national 13.8%, US 64.43%, and "other" 21.75%. This inflated last statistic was due to two "pan-Atlantic" features counted as British: the latest James Bond and romantic comedy *Notting Hill*, which cast Julia Roberts in the undemanding role of a Hollywood star on location in London.

The relatively small size of the Mexican market is seen from the Observatory's statistics for Latin America. While Mexico's population is more than double that of Spain (100 million to 39 million), its GDP is lower, as are its cinema admissions (120 million to the Spanish 131) and, overwhelmingly, its feature production which fluctuates alarmingly from 3 (1996), to 15 (1997), to 7 (1998). Interestingly, however, while Mexico's figure for admissions per inhabitant might seem low at 1.2 compared to cinephile Spaniards' 3.36 (one of the highest in Europe), Mexicans remain the keenest filmgoers in Latin America. Mexico also has the greatest number of screens on the continent, exceeding more populous Brazil by a considerable margin. Moreover attendance grew in Mexico by 7% compared to the previous year. It is clear, then, that in spite of differences in scale, Spain and Mexico have much in common, with cinemagoing more frequent, more profitable, and faster growing at home than in neighbouring nations.

Let us move now to the regulatory frameworks that serve, still, to frame these commercial trends. The European Union's Film Forum met in Strasbourg in 2000, after hosting a conference on cooperation between Europe and Latin America. The opening statement for this meeting of professionals was a reminder of the audiovisual trade deficit between the EU and the US: 7 billion euros in 1998 (European Film Forum, 1). While the topic for the round table was "Globalization and Cultural Diversity," the watchwords were distinctly European: "film heritage" and "quality cinema." A proposed Cinema Directive made such preconceptions clear:

Cultural identity is the common reference of the members of a community or of a nation and the essential base of their democratic choices; any breach of the cultural or linguistic identity of a community shall be susceptible [sic] to affect the founding principle of the Union. (*ibid.*, 12)

Or again:

The underscoring of the common cultural heritage justifies the organization, in each member state, of the collection and conservation of all films by the creation of a compulsory deposit. (*ibid.*, 13)

If film is assumed, immediately, to reflect a cultural or linguistic identity that deserves and requires preservation (with the statutory deposit signaling the heritage model with a vengeance), then the definition of "European cinematographic works" is more problematic. On the one hand, and in keeping with the familiar argument of "cultural exception," films "which are characterized by a high level of creativity and originality, cannot be considered as interchangeable or substitutable goods from the point of view of the consumer and must be treated in accordance with their specificity" (*ibid.*, 14). On the other hand, the necessary conditions for achieving such transcendent status are embarrassingly concrete, even mechanical. "European films" must be spoken in one of the languages of the EU (with the exception of "any parts of the dialogue which the screenplay requires to be in another language"); and they must achieve at least 15 points on a scale of 19, calculated on the basis of the nationalities of those creators, performers, and technicians who contribute to the production. Thus a director or "first role" scores a high 3, a screenwriter or "second role" a middling 2, and a set designer or shooting location a lowly 1.

As expected, perhaps, co-production is a particular problem here. Veteran auteur Werner Herzog complained in his intervention that EU rules prevented him from filming a brief sequence of the unique fauna in Easter Island (European Film Forum, 24). Council of Europe guidelines (Council of Europe electronic sources) specify that to be eligible for the once generous state support known as "advance on receipts" a partner in a co-production cannot exceed 80% or be lower than 10% of total budget. However, Eurimages, the funding body of which Spain is a member, made changes in 2000, dividing the competition into two separate schemes: "one for films with real circulation potential; one for films reflecting the cultural diversity of European cinema." While officials claimed that "the intention is not to support commercial films on the one hand and cultural films on the other," the selection criteria are clearly differentiated: "the first scheme assesses the commercial potential of a project," the second focuses on "a project's artistic and cultural value." Curiously enough the criteria are "less strict" in the second, art house category. While the Council grandly announces "a new philosophy" ("the main change [is] the emphasis on the film's effective financing and commitments"), its attached list of projects is less than inspiring, including as it does such disappointing co-productions as, on the "commercial" side, Fernando Trueba's *El embrujo de Shanghai* (Spain-France) and, on the "cultural" side, Ventura Pons' English-language *Food of Love* (Spain-Germany). Fernando Pino Solanas' *Afrodita, el sabor del amor* is the only Hispano-American project listed, matching Argentina with no fewer than four European countries, including Spain.

Spain's position is clearly anomalous here, keen as it is to establish cultural and commercial links with Latin America, an ambition not always aided by EU inflexibility over funding. Yet Madrid's audiovisual legislation betrays the same tensions between culture and commerce that we have seen in Brussels and Strasbourg. The law to support and promote cinema of 9 July 2001 echoes European tropes. It begins:

La creación cinematográfica y audiovisual es parte destacada de la cultura y tiene una importancia decisiva en el mantenimiento de la diversidad cultural. El cine presenta en la sociedad actual una dimensión cultural de primera magnitud, no sólo como patrimonio, también como proyección de nuestro país en el exterior, como expresión de su personalidad, de sus historias, formando parte de la identidad viva de un país ... Como forma reconocida de expresión informativa, documental, y creativa, es obligación velar por la conservación de las obras cinematográficas y audiovisuales y crear cauces e incentivos para que su desarrollo sea posible ...

Audiovisual and film production is an outstanding part of culture and has a decisive importance in the maintenance of cultural diversity. Cinema has a cultural dimension of the first magnitude in contemporary society, not just as a form of cultural heritage, but as the projection of our country abroad and as an expression of its personality and its histories, thus forming part of its living identity ... As an acknowledged form of informational, documentary, and creative expression, there is an obligation to preserve works of cinema and other audiovisual forms and to create channels and incentives for their development ...

Cultural identity is downplayed, however, in the decree issued just a year later (14 June 2002). Here changes in funding aim to establish incentives for independent production houses and measures to ensure their competitiveness. While "cultural diversity" is mentioned once more (clearly in its European meaning of "state resistance to US hegemony"), more significant is the creation of a Comité de Análisis y Seguimiento del Mercado (Committee for Market Tracking and Analysis) whose role is to ensure industrial "transparency." Moreover the decree states explicitly that this reform of regulations is prompted by co-productions, which call into question the national identity of cinematic works, the main criterion cinema has been required to preserve at home and to project abroad.

In fact attempts to construct a transatlantic regulatory regime had been made throughout the 1990s. A veritable alphabet soup of acronyms came into being after CACI (the Conferencia de Autoridades Cinematográficas de Iberoamérica) established a film fund in 1989. The aim of the programme, baptized Ibermedia, was to construct an "Iberoamerican visual space" through training and distribution, as well as co-production. Of the thirteen original countries of CACI, seven established the Unidad Técnica Ibermedia (UTI) to coordinate a production slate over the period 1998–2002. In its first year Ibermedia lent financial support to 118 projects. These state funded initiatives overlapped with industry events, such as MIDIA (Mercado Iberoamericana de la Industria Audiovisual) (electronic sources), which in 1998 held its first "co-production market," also in Madrid.

A co-production agreement between Spain and Mexico had been drawn up as early as 1995, with the diplomatic aim of strengthening collaborative links ("fortalecer los lazos de colaboración") between the two countries. One precondition here for the greenlighting of projects is the approval of the two official film institutes (ICAA and IMCINE). In order to be considered a "national" picture in both countries (and thus to qualify for state subsidy) all projects are obliged to incorporate Mexicans and Spaniards at the level of both cast and crew, preferably in proportion to the percentage of funding offered by each country: "En principio, la aportación de cada pais incluirá, por lo menos, un elemento considerado como creativo, un actor en papel principal y un actor en papel secundario o un técnico cualificado" ("In principle the contribution of each country will include at least one element held to be creative, one actor in a starring role and one in a supporting role, and a qualified technician"). While no points system exists as in the European scheme, elements such as the shooting location are specified. Studios and lab facilities must also be within the territory of the majority partner in the project. State prestige, such as the attribution of national origin at festivals (will a feature be billed as Mexican-Spanish or Hispano-Mexican?), thus rubs shoulders with industrial protectionism (employment opportunities for actors and technicians) in the conflictive quest to create a common audiovisual space.

It is perhaps no surprise that film legislation enacted by successive Mexican presidents parallels the progressive commercialization of its Spanish counterparts. As late as 1998 the Salinas government's Ley Federal de Cinematografía still began by stressing that film is "un vehículo de expresión artística y educativa, y constituye una actividad cultural primordial, sin menoscabo del aspecto comercial que le es característico" ("a vehicle for artistic and educational expression, without denigrating the commercial aspect which is characteristic of it"). It went on to define film production as:

una actividad de interés social ... por expresar la cultura mexicana y fortalecer los vínculos de identidad nacional entre los diferentes grupos que la conforman. Por tanto, el Estado fomentará su desarrollo para cumplir su función de fortalecer la composición pluricultural de la nación mexicana. (Salinas electronic sources)

an activity of importance to society ... because it expresses Mexican culture and strengthens the ties of national identity amongst the various groups that make up the nation. The State will therefore encourage its development with the aim of strengthening the multicultural composition of the Mexican nation.

This gesture towards multiculturalism (in the US sense), comparable to the Spanish mention of the plural "histories" of the nation, is undermined, however, by the requirement that children's and educational films, the only foreign features not subtitled, must be dubbed within Mexico in order to preserve "national linguistic identity."

Three years later Vicente Fox signed a new *Reglamento* of the same law (Fox electronic sources). While protectionism is still present (with exhibitors required to observe a 10% quota for "national" films), the culturalist language of artistic expression and social benefit is generally omitted. One exception is the requirement that a copy of all Mexican features be lodged with the Cineteca, which continues to serve as a European-style repository of national heritage.

Now it seems only fair to mention at this point a representative product of the regulatory regime that immediately preceded the so-called Mexican renaissance. *El coronel no tiene quien le escriba* (*No one Writes to the Colonel*) of 1999 is a Mexican-Spanish-French co-production funded by no fewer than eight public and private sources including IMCINE and the Centre Nationale de la Cinématographie. Based of course on a prestigious source text by García Márquez, it is directed by Arturo Ripstein, one of the few Mexican auteurs to have built up a substantial and distinctive body of work over several decades. In accordance with the various state regulations, it features a multinational cast, boasting Mexican Salma Hayek and Spaniard Marisa Paredes in the main female roles. Decorative in mise en scène, stately in pace, and accepted for official competition at Cannes, *El coronel* has "quality" stamped all over it. Indeed one of its funding bodies is El Fondo para la Producción Cinematográfica de Calidad (Fund for Quality Film Production). Yet it was a commercial and, arguably, artistic disappointment, failing to find an audience. If European co-productions have long been reviled as "Europuddings," and UK films destined for the US market newly dismissed as "Nato-puddings," then *El coronel* is perhaps a "tortilla soup," with distinctly Colombian, Mexican, or Spanish ingredients stirred into an undifferentiated and undistinguished "Ibermedian" brew.

I will argue later that the casting of a foreign female star persists problematically in recent Mexican films of wholly "national" production. What is important here is to note that this traffic in women has become identified with the proverbially deracinated and despised co-production. *El País* (16 November 2001) writes of young actress Natalia Verbeke, whose "perfecto, castizo, inequívoco, y bien entonado español" ("perfect, pure, error free, and well spoken Spanish") in real life contrasts with her "elles arrastradas" ("slurred double Ls") in Buenos Aires-set *El hijo de la novia* (*Son of the Bride*): "no es el típico papel de española camuflada en un país latinoamericano, artimaña que siempre delata la coproducción escondida detrás" ("it's not the typical role where a Spanish woman is camouflaged for the part of a Latin American, a piece of deception that always betrays the co-production hidden behind") (electronic sources). Authentic and undubbed, she is as "local" as her

Argentine colleagues. Linguistic and cultural purity is celebrated here, even as the Spanish journalist takes pride in an actress who has managed to "hacer las Américas (Latinas)."

Continuing this gendered rhetoric, a territory report by *Screen International* in February 2002 names Mexico "the darling of Latin America." According to the correspondent, Mexican cinema has indeed revived in all three areas of production (with market share rising from 3% to 20%), distribution (with local companies spending unprecedented sums on prints and advertising), and exhibition (with old and unattractive theatres renewed for a wealthier and more educated audience). This change has coincided with the decline of the old statist model of protection-preservation: for the first time private investment has exceeded public support. The renaissance is, however, dependent on a small number of successful titles, especially *Amores perros* and *Y tu mamá también*, both of which were fully funded from private Mexican sources.

From protection to promotion: *Amores perros* and *Y tu mamá también*

I would like to begin my case studies of these films by advancing a number of propositions about them, which are widely accepted but somewhat paradoxical. First, both films are unqualified successes, both artistically (at festivals) and commercially (at the international box office), qualities which, as we have seen from government regulation, are often held to be mutually exclusive. Second, they are films held to be representative of their national origin (*Screen International* calls its survey "New Mexico"), yet they are openly indebted to US narrative genres (the intricate, interlocking structure of *Pulp Fiction* and the apparently casual episodic form of the road movie, respectively). Thirdly, they are films that openly display their break with the past ("New Mexico", once more) in relation to both state subsidy and the PRI identified art cinema of, say, Ripstein, yet they still aspire to recognition from the establishment (*Amores* won multiple Ariels; *Y tu mamá también* excluded itself from consideration as a protest against the lack of transparency in the voting process). Finally, the two films boast both of their private funding and of the artistic freedom allowed their directors. This neatly reverses the European or PRI-ista protection-promotion model whereby only state intervention could guarantee the creative liberty of smaller nations whose artistic heritage is believed to be threatened by mercenary US capitalism.

Clearly directors such as González Iñárritu and Cuarón no longer view their relationship with the US in the antagonistic terms of earlier Mexican directors. Both have loudly proclaimed (with Guillermo del Toro) their refusal to be confined to a Latin ghetto and their freedom to travel to realize their projects. If we step back a minute from the films themselves, however, we can examine the corporate ethos of new producers AltaVista and Anhelo in relation to their parent companies, CIE and Omnilife.

The stated aims of both AltaVista and Anhelo are to combine artistic innovation with commercial viability, in a way that statist regulation has found impossible, even as it now struggles to make national audiovisual industries more competitive. This is how AltaVista presents itself on its modest website:

Altavista films fundada en 1999 está dedicada a la producción de películas dirigidas al público de habla hispana. Se crea a partir del creciente interés del público nacional de verse reflejado en las producciones del país; esto se ha modificado a través del tiempo ya que el cambio completo y radical de la infraestructura de la exhibición ha cambiado la demografía cinéfila de nuestro país ... Altavista Films ... ha logrado ser una opción real y viable para cualquier cineasta interesado en hacer una película de calidad internacional en México.

Altavista Films, set up in 1999, is dedicated to the production of films aimed at a Spanish-speaking audience. It has been created in the light of the growing interest of the domestic audience in seeing itself reflected in the productions made in this country. This has changed over time given that the total and radical change in exhibition infrastructure has changed the demography of filmgoers in this country ... Altavista Films ... has come to represent a real, viable option for any filmmaker interested in producing a film of international quality in Mexico.

Likewise in *Amores perros*' stylish press kit, distributed at Cannes, executive producer Martha Sosa describes the young company in the following terms: "a new option to produce high quality films in Mexico aimed at box-office success." What is striking here is the stress on the local, both in production and reception. Altavista's target is a Mexican and Spanish-speaking audience which wishes to recognize itself on screen; but this public is understood not in the abstract or ideal terms of state diplomacy but in direct relation to the new demographic that frequents the recently upgraded cinemas. If, as in Spain, filmgoing became in the course of the 1990s a more socially select activity, then it makes both commercial and artistic sense to aim for "quality," here redefined problematically in relation to box office. Any international audience, seduced perhaps by these higher production values, is cited only as an afterthought. The localist philosophy extends to funding: Altavista features were intended to cover their modest budgets in the Mexican market and five out of the first seven were indeed successful at home, an impressive track record.

There is a broader context, however. Altavista's parent company is Estudio México, which is in turn a part of CIE. *Amores perros*' producers exploited the potential of "vertical integration" which is proudly announced on CIE's website as the secret of the corporation's success. The biggest live entertainment company in Mexico, CIE not only arranges tours by, say, the Rolling Stones. It also owns the stadiums in which they play, the franchise which sells the tickets, and even the provision of drinks consumed during the concert. Likewise little Altavista enjoyed the synergy of its sibling companies Nuvisión, the distributor of *Amores perros*, and CIE's musical subsidiaries, which marketed the soundtrack and staged concerts by bands featured in the film. Trailers ran on video screens in Hard Rock Cafes, another CIE associate. Promotion also relied heavily on González Iñárritu's own professional background in the three areas of radio, television, and advertising. This professionalization of marketing is not only impossible to achieve through statist bureaucracy. It is also one of the three commercial criteria often held to distinguish and disadvantage national cinemas in comparison with Hollywood, the others being the absence of a viable star system and the lack of involvement by producers in the creative process.

Intentionally or not, Altavista fulfilled all three criteria. Cannily marketed in Mexico (exploiting foreign festival success to enhance domestic expectation), *Amores perros* also launched Gael García as the unchallenged young cinematic idol; and its producer Sosa is actively involved in seeking out and shaping new projects. Less obvious is the transatlantic factor here. CIE now operates in Argentina,

Brazil, Colombia, Chile, and Spain. And Estudio México and Nuvisión recently launched a US offshoot, aiming to distribute films from both Latin America and Spain in association with Spanish media conglomerate PRISA.

The parent company of Anhelo, fledgling producer of *Y tu mamá también*, also has this "triangular" business base. The home page of Omnilife (motto "Gente que cuida a la gente" ["People who look after people"]) features thumbnails of the flags of the nine Latin American countries, plus those of the US and Spain, in which its nutritional supplements are distributed. Populist CEO Jorge Vergara, executive producer with Cuarón of *Y tu mamá también*, smartly casual in a black suit and no tie, welcomes visitors to the site, pitching products that will "change the lives" of Iberoamerican consumers through Omnilife's proclaimed combination of ancient herbal tradition and nutritional high tech. Just one of a dozen subsidiaries of the voracious Omnilife, Anhelo has, like Altavista, opted for "quality," with its excellent second feature, Guillermo del Toro's *El espinazo del diablo* (*The Devil's Backbone*), being described as a coproduction with the "award-winning Spanish director Pedro Almodóvar." Like CIE, Omnilife cannily markets the engaging and diverse soundtrack of its successful feature under yet another newly formed subsidiary, Suave.

If *Amores perros'* press brook called attention to the joint goal of quality and box office, *Y tu mamá también*'s stresses the artistic independence of its director from a very visible producer (Omnilife's website features lengthy clips of Vergara addressing employees at huge junkets). We are told that "Jorge has always guaranteed Alfonso complete freedom as a director, the best production quality possible and freedom from interference or censorship." Yet the handsome version of the script published in Mexico tells another story. Vergara's frame is visible in a large number of location shots, both in Mexico City at the start of the filming and on the fabled beach at its end (the film was shot in sequence). His name is also featured first in the credits. Moreover Vergara even got to play a minor part. Seen only from behind, he impersonates at an early wedding scene the Mexican president whose identity was not yet known, because of elections imminent at the time of shooting.

Whether Cuarón implied any irony in this piece of casting is unclear. Vergara's global ambitions are evident from Ominilife's website; and excerpts from its radio programming reveal such unsavoury sides to his business as the repeated denial of the existence of HIV and the claim that Omnilife's high tech herbal concoctions are a cure for AIDS. Whatever the case, there could be no clearer sign of the change of funding paradigm from public to private than the impersonation of the head of state by a pseudo-presidential chief executive officer. Moreover, Anhelo, like Altavista once more, has made its move into the magic triangle of Ibermedian production space. Cuarón and Vergara set up a new branch in New York under the name El Delirio (Delirio electronic sources). Cuarón explained: "Esta compañía tiene dos brazos: uno es América Latina y España para producir películas habladas en español; y otro es Los Angeles para producir películas internacionales no habladas en español" ("This company has two arms: one in Latin America and Spain for producing films in Spanish; and the other in Los Angeles for producing international films not made in Spanish"). It is a connection long desired, but unachieved, by state institutions keen to regulate co-production and thus create a common audiovisual market.

One future project is said to be a feature starring Spanish actress Aitana Sánchez Gijón. We have seen that the nationality of the featured cast was at once required by state regulatory regimes and decried by domestic audiences, wary of "inauthentic" tortilla soups. Why, then, did both *Amores perros* and *Y tu mamá también* continue to cast Spanish actresses as their female protagonists? One hundred per cent privately funded, they were free of government control; and directed primarily to domestic audiences in Mexico, they did not overtly court the Spanish public.

Let us examine a little closer Goya Toledo's supermodel Valeria in the first film (Figure 19) and Maribel Verdú's fugitive wife Luisa in the second (Figure 20). It is noteworthy that no attention is called within *Amores perros* to the nationality of Valeria. Described as "the Latin American representative" of perfume Enchant, she is clearly all too at home in the glamorous world of adulterous magazine editor Daniel and publicity seeking actor Andrés. While Goya Toledo makes no attempt to disguise her Peninsular accent and idiolect, there is only one point when her origin is remarked on: taken to hospital after the car crash, she begs Daniel not to get in touch with her father back in Spain, saying he is capable of saying she deserved this misfortune. Significantly, perhaps, the role of Valeria was the one most changed in the shooting and editing process. González Iñárritu consistently cuts planned sequences still in the final version of the script that would have directed more audience sympathy to this vain and superficial character. Thus we do not learn that Valeria has previously suffered an abortion of Daniel's child and we are not privy to scenes of domestic intimacy between the lovers (Daniel tenderly tending to the injured Valeria on the toilet) or charting the gradual disintegration of their relationship (a first argument after Valeria dismisses the maid brought in by Daniel to care for her). It is telling that Valeria is not provided with a back story in way that the other Mexican protagonists are: the personal histories of Gael García's Octavio, Emilio Echevarría's El Chivo, and indeed Alvaro Guerrero's Daniel are clearly laid out for the spectator, thus facilitating empathy and directing sympathy.

Maribel Verdú's Luisa is rather similar. Here the "Spanishness" of the character is more accentuated, since in dialogue sometimes suggested by the actress herself the Mexican boys are required to explain their ostentatiously local *chilango* (Mexico City) dialect. And while we are at times given privileged access to Luisa's emotional state (the audience, but not the boys, watches her tearful telephone breakup with her Mexican husband), much of her back story is again denied us, while the boys are fully established in their social and psychological context. A fully detailed biography of the character is only accessible to those who buy the lavish script published in Mexico (reproduced as a blurry booklet with the UK DVD). And while viewers may guess that Luisa is sick, it is only after her disappearance from the narrative that her terminal cancer is revealed. The excellent website pays almost no attention to the character, encouraging surfers to dress the twin *charolastras* in their grungy garments or tour their battered station wagon. As in *Amores perros*, then, there is a certain disengagement from or distancing of the Spanish character, one mitigated only by the subtlety of both performances. Moreover while the presence of Verdú, popular veteran of some thirty Spanish films, may have helped the marketing of *Y tu mamá también* in her native country, the relatively unknown Toledo would have given no such advantage to *Amores perros*.

What I would argue, then, is that this anomalous casting plays a similar role to the transatlantic or "triangular" ambitions of the films' twin production companies. The often ridiculed attempts at co-production made by government agencies are here rewritten in a local context, with transnational traffic at once acknowledged and disavowed by the presence of foreign actresses who are both spectacularly visible on screen and covertly undercut in the narrative. The fetish of Europeanness thus stands in for a globalization of the audiovisual industries which cannot be directly represented in films whose claim to authenticity is based on national specificity: both features were shot entirely on location and make much of their "natural" settings. The dangerous liaisons depicted in *Amores perros* and *Y tu mamá también* might then be read symptomatically as replaying the missed encounters of two cinematic suitors in the production arena: Mexico, the darling of Latin America, and Spain, the painted lady.

The ambivalent presentation of the Spanish actress we have seen in these two films is not universal. María Novaro's *Sin dejar huella* (*Without a Trace*, 2000) was made in the same year as *Amores perros* (although released in Spain in 2001) and was produced in part by the same company. In this case Altavista collaborated with Tornasol and Televisión Española to make a co-production that was 70% Mexican and 30% Spanish. A female road and buddy movie which features charismatic performances as attractive as those in *Amores perros* and photogenic locations the equal of *Y tu mamá también*, *Sin dejar huella* casts Aitana Sánchez Gijón as a well educated smuggler of Mayan antiquities who hooks up with a working-class woman fleeing the *maquiladoras* (export production plants) of the US border. In this case (often compared by critics to *Thelma and Louise*) the Spanish star is indeed provided with a back story and is treated sympathetically by the female Mexican director. It remains the case, however, that Novaro's feature was not a commercial success and achieved little international distribution. Trans-Atlantic traffic remained problematic in the cinematic arena.

How then do we theorize this conundrum? Clearly what we have witnessed is a shift, partial and incomplete, from a vestigial paradigm of protection-preservation (in which cinema embodies an endangered national identity and heritage) to an emergent promotion-innovation paradigm (in which art and commerce are no longer held to be antagonistic in the elaboration of a new national style). Ironically this second model, more friendly to US-style production practices (the star system, professional promotion, and producer involvement in the development process), can lead not to homogenization but to a reinforcement of territorial markers such as land and language. As Daniel Mato (2003) has recently argued of telenovela production based in Miami, "transnationalization and the globalization of consumption ... do not imply the deterritorialization of either" (196). My own microanalysis of production processes aims, like that of Mato, to disprove the "fallacy" of homogenization by revealing that "what we call globalization is in fact the result of numerous different social processes which arise specifically from the actions of particular social protagonists; numerous and diverse but nonetheless identifiable and thus open to investigation" (*ibid.*, 196). The complex interplay of such diverse agents as the EU and Intermedia, IMCINE and Anhelo, reveals that the generally accepted tendency to cultural homogenization is by no means self-evident.

Of course the two paradigms I have described overlap. The protectionist model can produce innovative filmmaking; the innovative model (as I have shown elsewhere in the case of *Amores perros* [Smith 2003] and *Y tu mamá también* [Smith electronic sources]) owes more than it cares to acknowledge to the filmic fathers it has so vehemently disavowed. Thus most recently the patriarch of Mexican cinema, Ripstein, has turned to the new medium of digital video, while free-marketeer Fox has announced a public programme to increase feature production to fifty a year. In Spain, meanwhile, plans drastically to cut state funding led insiders to predict, as on previous such occasions, the death of their industry. However, with even EU regulation turning in favour of industrial track records as a precondition for funding, the tide is running in the same direction on both sides of the Atlantic.

Perhaps Bourdieu's field theory is the best way of conceptualizing this situation. As the sum total of all operations in any given area, the field is made up of the intersection of texts, producers, and institutions. Moreover the field flexibly regulates social and cultural change by aligning people and things in an apparently natural order:

The specific regularities that constitute the economy of the field [are] immediately filled with sense and rationality for every individual ... hence the effect of communal validation which is the basis of collective belief in the game and its fetishes. (Bourdieu 1990, 66)

This is also known as "habitus:" the correlation of "objective probabilities and subjective aspirations" (*ibid.*, 54). According to Bourdieu, habitus serves to guarantee the constancy of practices better than "formal rules or explicit norms." It thus follows that in a new funding environment, new forms of filmmaking will arise with apparent spontaneity. Altavista and Anhelo see no contradiction between artistic freedom and commercial constraints. This is because the directors with whom they collaborate seek the freedom to make films that have good commercial prospects; or, to put it another way, the producers offer funding for films that exhibit the signs of artistic freedom. This is not to deny that such films can be genuinely innovative and hugely enjoyable. It is rather to suggest that innovation remains necessarily enclosed within the magic circle of habitus.

At moments of crisis the field will fracture and be reconfigured. Here is the chance for what Bourdieu calls the "allodoxia:" "an alternative system of taken for granted assumptions running counter to the implicit consensus" (Bourdieu 1979, 156). While their continuing controversies with the Academy over the Ariels and rating system remain symptomatic of this tension between paradigms, it seems likely that the licensed heretics González Iñárritu, Cuarón, and their friend and colleague Guillermo del Toro will become the new orthodoxy. This new alignment of aesthetics and economics is what lies behind a letter to *The Economist*, which claims that "after a decade of privatization the Mexican case shows that markets have better taste than bureaucracies" (26 October–1 November 2002). It is more likely that the Mexican renaissance is a prime example of the interaction between state, industry, and identity that has been so ably documented by Castells elsewhere.

Works cited

Amores perros. Cannes: Altavista, 2000 [press kit].

Bourdieu, Pierre. *The Inheritors*. Chicago: University of Chicago Press, 1979.

—. *The Logic of Practice*. Cambridge: Polity, 1990.

Castells, Manuel. *The Information Age, Volume 2: The Power of Identity*. Oxford: Blackwell, 2000.
Cuarón, Carlos and Cuarón, Alfonso. *Y tu mamá también: guión y argumento*. Guadalajara, no date.
European Audiovisual Observatory. *Focus 2000: World Film Market Trends*. Cannes, 2001.
Mato, Daniel. 'Transnationalization of telenovela production.' *Journal of Latin American Studies* 12, 2003.
Smith, Paul Julian. *Amores perros: Modern Classic*. London: BFI, 2003.

Specialist periodicals

The Economist (London)
Screen International (London)
Variety (Los Angeles)

Electronic sources

All accessed 17 October 2002
Acuerdo de coproducción:
    www.cinespain.com/ICAA/legisl/ conven/mexico1.html
Altavista: www.cie-mexico.com.mx/espanol/cie340/i/
    altavista.htm
CIE: www.cie-mexico.com.mx/espanol/cie3100.htm
Cine por la red:
    www.porlared.com/cinered/noticiasn_act0 2022702.html
Council of Europe:
    www.jurisint.org/pub/01/en/doc/218_2.htm
Delirio:
    www.estacioncentral.com/cine/cinemexicano/mexican.htm
Estudio Mexico Prisa:
    www.estacioncentral.com/cine/cinemexicano/mexican.htm
European Film Forum: www.forum-eurocine.com/2000_gb.pdf
Fox:
    http://imcine.gob.mex/dream/html/reglamento_ley_fed.html
Hijo de la novia: http://tentaciones.elpais.es/t/d/20011116/
    temaport/tp0.htm
Ibermedia: www.oei.es/ibermedia.htm

MIDIA: http://pymes.tsai.es/midia/mercado.html

Noticias:
http://noticias.juridicas.com/base_datos/Admin/rd526–2002.html

Omnilife:
http://200.34.37.225/home/productos/introduccion.htm

Salinas: http://imcine.gob.mex/dream/html/reglamento_ley_federal.html

Smith, Paul Julian. www.bfi.org.uk/sightandsound/2002_04/heaven.html

Toda la ley. www.todalaley.com/mostrarLey434p.1tn.htm

Y tu mamá también. www.YTuMamaTambien.com

Index:

Page numbers in *italics* refer to illustrations in the text